LEBANON TO GHANA

THE FOOD I GREW UP WITH

LEBANON TO GHANA

THE FOOD I GREW UP WITH

Robert Bousamra

Big Sky Publishing Pty Ltd

PO Box 303, Newport, NSW 2106, Australia

Phone: 1300 364 611

Fax: (61 2) 9918 2396

Email: info@bigskypublishing.com.au

Web: www.bigskypublishing.com.au

Cover design, photography, and typesetting: Robert Bousamra

Printed in China through Asia Pacific Offset Limited

National Library of Australia Cataloguing-in-Publication entry (pbk)

Author: Bousamra, Robert.

Title: Lebanon to Ghana : the food I grew up with / Robert Bousamra.

ISBN: 9781922132086 (pbk.)

Subjects: Bousamra, Robert.
        Food habits--Ghana.
        Food habits--Lebanon.
        Cooking, Lebanese.
        Cooking, Ghanaian.

Dewey Number: 641.595692

National Library of Australia Cataloguing-in-Publication entry (ebook)

Author: Bousamra, Robert.

Title: Lebanon to Ghana [electronic resource] : the food I grew up with / Robert Bousamra.

ISBN: 9781922132093 (ebook)

Subjects: Bousamra, Robert.
        Food habits--Ghana.
        Food habits--Lebanon.
        Cooking, Lebanese.
        Cooking, Ghanaian.

Dewey Number: 641.595692

BIG SKY PUBLISHING
www.bigskypublishing.com.au

*'If you do not have leftovers,
you have not cooked enough'.*

Acknowledgements

*I dedicate this book to my family and would like to give thanks to all
the wonderful people who have inspired and helped me create this
book. I give special thanks to my mother Yvonne, my sister Hayat
and my good friend Elizabeth Woolnough, for all their wonderful
advice. A special thank you goes out to Les Flood for providing
props for the game meat section photographs.*

Book written, designed and photographed by Robert Bousamra.

Contents

My Cooking History

Growing up in an extended Lebanese family, my love of food started early. Food was always central to gatherings of family and friends. In preparing food for our family, my mother showed me that fresh and flavoursome food was not only healthy, it was something to be shared and enjoyed. This cookbook is a collection of the much-loved family recipes from my childhood, which are not only a product of my traditional Lebanese background, but influenced by the cultures of places we lived - Ghana and Australia.

My grandparents on my mother's side migrated to Ghana from Lebanon with their children. They raised their children in Ghana and travelled backwards and forwards to Lebanon for holidays to visit relatives. It was on one of these trips that my mother met my father, a hairdresser working in Lebanon. They married in Ghana, where he set up a hair salon soon after moving there. My brother and I were both born in Ghana while my sister was born in Lebanon.

Growing up in Africa in the 1960s was an adventure, and the richness of the culture and the geography impacted on our lifestyle in many ways. A coastal country positioned on the fertile equatorial belt, Ghana produces tropical foods including yams, cassava, corn, peanuts, mangoes and coconuts and the main exports include timber, cocoa, palm oil, kola nut, coffee and gold. Ghana at that time was very tribal, with the main tribe being Ashanti, a matrilineal society who are famous for their handicrafts, weaving, wood carving, pottery and metallurgy. Crafted items included hand-carved stools, fertility dolls and colourful woven kente cloth, and were primarily made by the men.

The Ghanaian diet is predominantly made up of starchy vegetables served with soup or a sauce. The soup would usually include seasonal vegetables or whatever meat was available at the time - mostly fish, chicken and goat. Lamb and beef were mostly imported from milder grazing countries more suited to cattle farming.

The Ghanaian people had many joyous celebrations and festivities that were full of music and dance.

They loved music and any chance they could they would bring out their drums and string instruments and start singing and dancing. For a young boy it was magical and has instilled in me a great love of music.

As a child I was never bored. My cousin and I would play at my uncle's timber yard, the workers would cut out toy guns made from timber and we would play 'cops and robbers or 'cowboys and Indians' running and hiding in the surrounding grounds and mounds of saw dust. I remember sitting in mango trees. eating sweet ripe mangos, or catching mud crabs in the nearby mangroves. Between my cousins and the local children, there was always something to do and someone to play with. These were very interesting times but sometimes very frightening.

The Ghanaian people had their own traditional spiritual system with many deities that they could call on when needed. They believed in a magic system sometimes referred to as 'juju' and would practise these rituals and ceremonies in the villages and town centres. One such event was the 'trial by magic' where a man accused of committing a crime would be tried by the spiritual leader using magic. The ritual involved placing two long poles balanced on the shoulders of his two assistants. The accused would stand sideways between the poles and be questioned by the priest. If he told a lie the poles would reportedly move and close in on his chest indicating a guilty verdict. As children we were not allowed to witness these events but tales of their existence would keep our young imaginations entertained for years.

In Ghana the food culture was an integral part of our lifestyle. We lived very close to an extended family of uncles, aunts, grandparents and many cousins, so a family gathering was always a feast. Even visiting the markets with my mother was a culinary experience. While shopping at the markets, we would buy lunch from hot food vendors selling chichinga, beef or sausage kebabs, kelewele, fried plantain with ginger and peanuts, jollof rice wrapped in banana leaf and a variety of sweet cakes and donuts. My mum learnt many of the local popular dishes and

would cook them at home as additions to the Lebanese food she usually cooked, or as a main meal. The recipes were never altered; if my mother was cooking a Lebanese meal it was made as she always made it using traditional spices and ingredients, as was the Ghanaian food.

Lebanese food is very different from the local Ghanaian food we experienced, with the latter being more closely related to Greek and Italian style cooking, using similar ingredients found around the Mediterranean with spice influences from the Middle East, Europe and North Africa. On the weekends we would have a large gathering for lunch at my uncle's house. My mother and aunty would prepare food to feed twelve people and always made extra for any unexpected guests. There was always plenty of food left over, and that was what inspired me to coin the phrase, 'if you do not have left overs you have not cooked enough.' The influence of Ghanaian cooking on my mother's style of Lebanese cooking was not so much a cross fertilisation of recipes but an integration of whole recipes. For example, in a typical mezza

spread my mother would include some of the Ghanaian finger foods such as chichinga or kelewele alongside our typical spread of dips and finger food.

Hunting was a past-time shared by men on the weekends. It was not seen as a sport where animals were shot just for the sake of it, the men shot only what they needed and knew could be eaten. The men enjoyed being outdoors walking and talking, seeing the landscape and enjoying the fresh air. They would shoot and bring home quail, rabbit, hare, duck and deer. The game meat would be shared among family and friends. Weekends were a time for everyone to get together, and living so close to our extended family, it felt like there was a party every weekend. The ladies would prepare plenty of food for everyone and if there was any game meat from the hunt, that would be cooked on a wood fired barbecue, alongside lamb or chicken. There would always be music playing in the background with lots of talking, joking, laughing, drinking and eating.

In 1970, when I was six years old, nearly seven, my family migrated to Adelaide because of political

unrest in Ghana. My parents chose Australia as it was seen as a better place to bring up children, particularly those who had already started an English education. My uncle and his family decided to stay in Ghana and carry on working and growing his timber and hardware business. I still have a strong memory of the morning we left Ghana. It was still dark and very early. I remember waking up and being confused as to why we had to get up so early. We arrived in Adelaide on a windy day in September 1970 and we were met by a good friend of my uncle who took us to a hotel. It wasn't long before we settled in and started to make some wonderful new friends.

We had a great house with lots of fruit trees, including almonds, figs and a big grapevine. We had good neighbours who we would swap home grown fruit and vegetables with. Two doors down lived an Italian family who had a daughter my age. The two of us played together and her mother thought I was wonderful – she thought she had met her future son-in-law and always wanted to feed me. This was where I first discovered Italian food and the wonderful world of pasta, pizza and other famous Italian dishes.

After two years my, family moved to Leichhardt in New South Wales and eventually moved again and settled in the western Sydney suburb of Auburn. Auburn is a great multicultural suburb with a large proportion of Lebanese and Turkish people. I made friends with Turkish, Spanish and Italian boys from my school who – like Lebanese people – are natural born 'foodies'. My teenage years were a varied culinary experience, eating at my home and the homes of my friends. All this diversity, together with my mum's cooking, was what further inspired my interest in food and led me to explore other cuisines. With the help of my brother and sister I began cooking as a teenager and learning my mother's family recipes and developing my own cooking skills.

The recipes in this book are the authentic, traditional Lebanese recipes passed down by my family, together with a selection of Ghanaian inspired dishes from my childhood. You will find that the recipes in this book are not a hard and fast formula, but a combination of ingredients that work together. The quantities of each ingredient can change depending on the mood of the person cooking as well as the particular combination of dishes being served. One day you may decide to make the sauce a little richer and spicier and this is fine, as long as the most important thing is maintained – the balance of flavours and the requirements of your guests. Make sure you always use top quality, fresh ingredients though as this is essential to creating beautiful flavours.

The next section of the book explains some basic ingredients and methods that are the foundations of Lebanese cooking, such as spices, herbs, dried grains and legumes and some prepared ingredients – the common items you would find in the pantry and refrigerator of a Lebanese cook.

Basic ingredients

Tomato Paste

Lebanese food has many dishes that use concentrated tomato paste. It is important to have a good quality, rich, concentrated tomato paste in your pantry. The supermarket brands are not rich enough and you will need twice the normal amount when cooking. A good quality tomato paste is very dark in colour and thick in texture. You can purchase good quality Greek or Turkish pastes from a continental delicatessen or fine food outlet.

Chickpeas, Beans and Lentils

These three legumes are common to several recipes in Lebanese cuisine. It is always better to have a good supplier of legumes, such as a whole foods outlet or a fine food delicatessen, especially when buying the dried variety. When beans and chickpeas become too dry it will take several hours of cooking to get them to a soft, cooked stage. A good method is to soak the dry beans and chickpeas for a day and night in water with a teaspoon of baking soda prior to cooking. Change the water twice during this period and wash well before cooking. For convenience you can substitute the dry beans or chickpeas with the cooked canned variety, just make sure you select a good quality brand. This will reduce your cooking time. When you are cooking the dried variety always check that they are cooked by squeezing a bean between your fingers to make sure it is soft and tender.

Rice and Egg Noodles

These two ingredients are used to make Lebanese rice and are always in my pantry. The traditional rice Lebanese people cook with is the short grain variety, but long grain rice can be used instead. The egg noodles are browned in a little oil and the rice added and boiled using the evaporative method. This produces a lovely nutty flavour making a much more tasty and interesting rice.

The Meats

Lamb and Mutton

Lamb and mutton are the traditional meats used in Lebanese cooking. Mutton has the stronger flavour and is best suited for stewing or slow roasting dishes, whereas lamb cuts such as backstraps and leg are best used for quick cooking on a wood fire. Although mutton backstraps can make excellent shish-kebabs.

Minced Lamb

Minced lamb is now available at your supermarket or you can make your own by grinding the lamb using a hand-cranked meat grinder The grinders come in various sizes from large, medium and small.

Coarse Ground Lamb

To learn to make coarse ground lamb will probably take some practice using chef's knives. On a timber chopping board hold two chef's knives opposite to each other. The right hand holds the knife in a carving

grip pointing away from your body. The left hand holds the knife in a stabbing grip with the knife point pointing towards you. Bring the flat surfaces of the blades together over the meat. Create a scissor slicing action by sliding the blades past each other through the meat. Do this slicing motion until the right coarse consistency is achieved.

The Wood Fire

This is an essential part of Lebanese outdoor cooking. Everything we cook outdoors is done over an open wood fired grill. The wood fire imparts a smoky flavour as well as cooking tender meats by quickly sealing in the flavour. The wood fire should be allowed to burn down so that you have large

hot coals emitting a little smoke and plenty of heat. When you have the perfect fire, you should have an even distribution of hot glowing coals with short flames providing an even heat across the grill. The grill should not be heavy and closed but light and open so it does not absorb the heat and allows the fire to do the cooking.

Herbs and Spices

Lebanese food uses herbs and spices common to Mediterranean and near Eastern cooking. The word 'Baharat' means a combination of spices in Lebanese, derived from the word 'pepper'. In this section I explain the herbs and spices I grew up with and have used in this book, including their flavours and how they are used.

Salt, White and Black Pepper

There are a variety of salts to choose from, including rock salt, sea salt and vegetable salt. I recommend using a salt that is natural and free of additives such as rock or sea salt. Ground white pepper is hotter than black and commonly mixed with other spices or added while cooking.

Cinnamon

Cinnamon an ancient spice dating back to Biblical times. The name 'cinnamon' comes from the Phoenician language through its Greek interpretation. The spice comes from the bark of the cinnamon tree and has a sweet warm flavour. You can purchase it in its bark form or as a fine powder. My mother used cinnamon powder in sweet and savoury dishes.

Allspice (Pimento)

Allspice is another name for pimento. Ground pimento combines the characteristic flavour and aroma of cloves, nutmeg, cinnamon and pepper, all combined in one spice - hence the name allspice. It is used in its ground form combined with other spices and used with lamb and other red meats.

Nutmeg

Nutmeg is an ancient spice introduced to Europe by the Arabs, having a sweet - although not as sweet as cinnamon – spicy, warm flavour. It is used mostly in its ground form in Lebanese cooking. This spice combines well with cinnamon, allspice, white pepper and salt to make a lamb seasoning.

Anise (Yansoon)

Anise, ground or whole, is used in sweets and teas. Anise is used to flavour liquorice, but the spice is not as strong or sweet and is very herbaceous.

Sumac

Sumac is a red berry from the Rhus Coriaria plant and has a tangy astringent flavour. It is used in salads and seafood, and can also be used as a more interesting flavour to replace lemon. Sumac is also mixed with other herbs such as oregano, sesame seeds and olive oil to create dips and spreads.

Turmeric

Tumeric is a spice which is used to flavour sweet biscuits and savoury dishes. The biscuits my mother made are deep fried and glazed, dusted with sugar or simply left plain. Turmeric is also used as flavouring for rice and vegetable dishes.

Mint

Fresh mint is used in many dishes, from cold salads to hot dishes and goes especially well with yoghurt. Lebanese people will eat mint it in its fresh form with olives, yoghurt, cheese and other delicacies. Dried mint is also used in cooking when fresh mint is not available.

Oregano

Fresh oregano is used in salads whilst the dry herb is used in baking savoury dishes and to make a traditional dip. Like mint it is also eaten fresh, served with condiments and delicacies.

Continental Parsley (Italian Parsley)

This herb is the most used, especially when making Tabouleh. It is also used in salads, eaten fresh or mixed into other recipes. Every Lebanese house will have parsley growing in their garden, along with oregano and mint. Other favourite plants Lebanese people grow include grape vines, red or green chillies, lemon trees and in the right climate, almond and fig trees. When I was young I had all of these and more in my backyard.

These are the herbs and spices I grew up with and which I still use in my Lebanese cooking. There are many other more exotic herbs and spices used in other Lebanese recipes which are not listed here. Good quality spices are just as important to a recipe as fresh ingredients. Always look for the finest quality and store them properly so they keep fresh. Some spices you can buy in bulk and some you will need to replace more often as these quickly loose their freshness.

A hint when you are grinding fresh spices to use in recipes is to lightly toast them in a non-stick pan for 1-2½ minutes. This will release the oils and bring out the flavours. Be careful not to burn or overcook the spice and always give them a shake and a stir while you are toasting. Then put the spices in a mortar and pestle and grind them to the consistency you require for your recipe. By doing this you will get a stronger fuller flavour and aroma.

The basics

Pine nut mix

Ingredients

¾ cup pine nuts browned in olive oil (80 g)

2 large onions finely chopped (300 g)

2 level teaspoons salt (6 g)

2 level teaspoons white pepper (6 g)

2 level teaspoons ground allspice (6 g)

300 g coarse ground mutton or lamb (½ cup)

Some of the recipes in this book use a stuffing made from lamb and pine nuts and the ingredients listed here will make 500 grams of stuffing. The amount of stuffing you will need varies depending on the recipe you are making and you may need to make more or less, although 500 grams will be sufficient for most recipes. My mother would always make a larger batch and simply freeze the remaining amount.

Brown the pine nuts in a small amount of olive oil, stirring constantly until golden brown. When cooking the pine nuts you will need to be careful as they brown very quickly once the oil is hot and will continue browning once you take them off of the heat. Place the browned pine nuts on a plate and put aside.

In the same pan, brown the onion and meat in butter and olive oil, together with the spices, until the meat is brown and almost crispy. Then add the pine nuts, stir once or twice and take off the heat and put aside to use as a stuffing.

Toum *(garlic paste)*

Ingredients

4 large cloves of garlic (20 g)

1 level teaspoon coarse ground salt (3 g)

2-3 tablespoons extra virgin olive oil

With this recipe you can make as much garlic paste as you need or a larger amount to store in a sealed glass jar in the fridge. For a larger amount, double or triple the amount of ingredients.

To make the paste, place the ingredients in a mortar and pestle and grind until a smooth paste is formed. If you are making a larger amount to store for later, add around two to three tablespoons of extra virgin olive oil on top of the paste after you have put it in a jar. The oil will act as seal over the paste helping it last longer and stay fresher.

Lebanese rice

Ingredients

1 whole coil dry egg noodles (30 g)

2 cups long grain rice (400 g)

3 tablespoons olive oil

5 cups water (1 litre)

1 level teaspoon of salt (3 g)

Heat the olive oil in a saucepan and loosely break the egg noodles into the pan (crush the coil so that the strands are 1 to 2 inches long). Stir the noodles until golden brown and then add the water. Add the salt, and then stir the water at the same time adding the rice. Bring to a simmer and place the pot lid across the top of the saucepan leaving an opening for steam to escape. Stir occasionally and allow to cook until the water has evaporated. Take off the heat and allow to sit for 15 minutes.

Basic dough

Ingredients

3 cups plain flour sifted (480 g)

1 tablespoon dry baker's yeast (4 g)

1½ cups warm water (300 ml)

½ level teaspoon salt (1.5 g)

Mix the yeast in the warm water (make sure the water is not too hot otherwise it will kill the yeast) and let it sit in a warm place until bubbling. Mix the salt and the flour together then add the yeast, kneading until the dough is smooth and elastic with a shine. If the dough is too dry or too wet, add more water or flour. Cover the dough with a large tea towel and let it sit in a warm place and allow to double in size. Divide the dough into even portions and knead for 20-30 seconds. Form the dough into round balls and let rest for 30 minutes to 1 hour.

This dough can be used to make several of the recipes in this book, or baked as flat bread. To bake as bread, heat the oven to 240 degrees Celsius, and shape the balls of dough into thin flat rounds. Bake on a preheated flat tray for 3-5 minutes until the bread rises and is slightly brown on top. You can also use a bread machine set to basic dough to make this recipe. Change the 1¹/₂ cups of water to 1 cup of water and ¹/₂ cup of oil when making the dough for meat-filled pastries.

Home-made yoghurt

Ingredients

2 litres fresh milk (10 cups)

250 ml full cream natural set yoghurt

Small woollen blanket

Use the creamiest, all natural set yoghurt you can buy as it will make a difference. Pour the milk into a pot with a lid. Heat the milk to 85 degrees Celsius. Remove the pot from the heat and let it sit until the milk cools to 35 degrees Celsius. Stir in the natural yoghurt and put the lid on the pot. Wrap the pot in a woollen blanket and either place in your cool (turned off) oven or a dark cupboard overnight. This is to allow the milk to slowly cool allowing the culture to take hold. Check the pot the next morning and if the temperatures were correct you should have yoghurt.

There will be a certain amount of whey that you will need to drain from the top. You can do this by slowly and carefully pouring it from the pot. You can also use half of the yoghurt to make 'Labna' which is a thicker version of the yoghurt. To do this place half of the yoghurt in a muslin bag and hang over the sink for one to two hours. The whey will drip through the bag leaving a thick creamy yoghurt similar in consistency to cream cheese. The Lebanese call this 'Labna' and eat it as a dip with flat bread. It is served with a good quality virgin olive oil drizzled over the top.

Once you have prepared your yoghurt to the thickness you desire, place in a container and refrigerate. Your home-made yoghurt can be used to make the dips and salads as well as the yoghurt based-recipes shown later in this book.

Yoghurt sauce

Ingredients

½ cup fresh mint (15 g)

½ teaspoon garlic paste (3 g)

1 cup natural set yoghurt (200 ml)

Water

In a blender blend the yoghurt, garlic paste and mint until the mint has broken down into small specks. Add water, a little at a time, until the thickness is such that you can pour the sauce onto a plate and it should not run, similar to natural cream. Garnish the top with a sprinkle of cracked pepper and mint leaves.

Mint and garlic salad dressing

Ingredients

½ teaspoon garlic paste (3 g)

½ teaspoon rock salt (1.5 g)

1 level teaspoon whole black peppercorns (3 g)

¼ cup chopped mint (6 g)

40 ml fresh lemon juice

40 ml virgin olive oil

Place all the dry ingredients, including the mint, in a mortar and pestle and grind into a coarse paste, then add the lemon juice and olive oil. Mix well and decanter into a container to dress the salad just before serving.

Tahini dressing

Ingredients

1 cup stone ground tahini (220 g)

½ teaspoon garlic paste (3 g)

¼ level teaspoon rock salt (0.75 g)

40 ml fresh lemon juice

1 cup water

Place all the ingredients into a blender and add 1 cup of water. Blend until a nice rich thick sauce is achieved. If you need to add more water, salt or tahini, adjust the sauce accordingly to taste..

Fresh salads

Tabouleh

Ingredients

½ cup cracked wheat (60 g)

4 cups finely chopped parsley (120 g)

½ cup chopped mint (15 g)

1 cup finely chopped onion (130 g)

2 cups finely chopped tomatoes (320 g)

80 ml fresh lemon juice

60 ml extra virgin olive oil

1 level teaspoon allspice (3 g)

1 level teaspoon white pepper (3 g)

½ level teaspoon salt (1.5 g)

In warm water soak the cracked wheat for no more than 1-2 minutes then strain through a sieve. Squeeze the cracked wheat dry with your hands and place in a bowl. In a large mixing bowl bring together and mix all the ingredients except for the oil and lemon juice. Add half the lemon juice, half the extra virgin olive oil, all the spices, and mix and taste. The salad should be spicy, tangy and glistening with oil. Add the remaining oil to achieve the right glistening presentation and put into a serving bowl. Serves 3-4 people.

Potato and coriander salad

Ingredients

5 cups diced cooked potatoes (600 g)

1½ cups chopped coriander leaves (45 g)

½ teaspoon garlic paste (3 g)

½ level teaspoon rock salt (1.5 g)

80 ml lemon juice

60 ml extra virgin olive oil

Select your favourite potatoes suitable for boiling (a waxy potato such as Nicola or Kipfler). Wash, peel and boil the potatoes until tender, but not overcooked. Dice the potatoes into 1.5 cm cubes and put aside to cool. Crush the garlic and rock salt into a paste or use a garlic paste prepared earlier. In a large bowl bring together the potatoes, garlic paste, lemon juice, olive oil and coriander leaves. Toss well and garnish with black pepper. Taste and add more lemon juice or olive oil to suite your taste. Serves 3-4 people.

Fattoush

Ingredients

½ cup mint leaves picked whole (15 g)

1 small red onion, sliced into thin half rings (80 g)

1 large tomatoe, sliced into half moons (120 g)

2-3 cups coarsely cut cos lettuce (90 g)

1 medium sized Lebanese cucumber (150 g), sliced into half moons

80 ml fresh lemon juice

60 ml extra virgin olive oil

1 round of Lebanese bread, halved and toasted

1 level tablespoon sumac (10 g)

This is a salad full of colour and fragrance. Make sure you use the freshest of lettuce, mint, tomato and cucumber. This salad should look vibrant, crisp and taste absolutely fabulous. Also use a very good quality first cold pressed olive oil.

Peel the Lebanese bread apart separating the two sections and toast in an oven until golden brown. These will be used as the croutons for the salad.

In a bowl mix the chopped cos lettuce, tomato, onion, mint and cucumber. Crumble the bread into corn chip size pieces and mix into the salad. Sprinkle the sumac over the salad and drizzle the lemon juice and extra virgin olive oil and then toss the salad. You can also add more green ingredients such as parsley and chopped shallots.

An alternative method for the croutons is to make small toasted spirals from Lebanese flat bread. To do this rub olive oil onto the inside of the separated rounds of the bread using a basting brush. Sprinkle the sumac over the bread and rub in using the basting brush. Slice the bread into thin strips of 1 to 1.5 cm thick. Then curl the strips into loose spirals and hold together with a tooth pick. Toast in an oven until golden brown. When cold remove the tooth picks and toss the spirals into the salad. Using this method you will only need to add a very light sprinkle of sumac to the salad as the toasted spirals already have been coated with the spice.

Using the spiced and toasted spirals adds a gourmet touch to the salad which should impress your guests and is also a great way to carry the flavour of the sumac. Serves 3-4 people.

Oregano salad

Ingredients

3 cups picked oregano leaves (120 g)

1 cup finely chopped onion (130 g)

1 cup finely chopped tomato (160)

50 ml fresh lemon juice

50 ml extra virgin olive oil

¼ level teaspoon salt (0.75 g)

This is a very simple, easy and quick salad to make. It was a big favourite with my parents who always served it with kebbe or kebabs for Saturday lunches. My father liked it as a starter with a glass of Arak, before the main meal was cooked.

My father devoted his spare time to growing vegetables, herbs and making furniture from timber. We always had most of the herbs we needed and in summertime plenty of tomatoes and cucumbers. This salad brings back memories of freshly picked herbs and tomatoes.

In a bowl mix all the ingredients and season with oil and lemon juice, enough to be tangy but not wet enough so as to drown the salad. Serve this with Lebanese bread as a starter or a side salad with the baked or barbecued lamb. Serves 3-4 people.

Herb salad

Ingredients

2 cups coarsely chopped parsley (60 g)

2 cups picked oregano leaves (60 g)

1 cup rocket (30 g)

1 cup coarsely chopped fresh mint leaves (30 g)

1 cup finely chopped onion (130 g)

1½ cups diced Lebanese cucumber (180 g)

1½ cups diced roma tomato (240 g)

50 ml lemon fresh lemon juice

50 ml extra virgin olive oil

¼ level teaspoon salt (0.75 g)

A personal recipe inspired by the Oregano Salad but with more fresh fragrant herbs. This salad goes well with any barbecued lamb, chicken or fish. Very easy to make, just toss together all the dry ingredients and dress the salad using olive oil and lemon juice just before serving. Serves 3-4 people.

Aubergine and capsicum salad

Ingredients

1 large aubergine (700 g)

3 large capsicums (690 g)

60 ml fresh lemon juice

80 ml extra virgin olive oil

1 teaspoon garlic paste (6 g)

¼ cup oregano leaves (7.5 g)

1 level teaspoon caraway seeds (3 g)

½ level teaspoon rock salt (1.5 g)

Black pepper, to taste

This is a mouth-watering smoky vegetable salad which is the perfect accompaniment to char-grilled lamb. It is a personal recipe of mine which I created after being inspired by my mother roasting eggplants. Once you have tried this salad you will make it one of your favourites.

Prepare the wood fire before you start preparing the vegetables. (If you do not have a wood fire you can use a gas BBQ to roast your vegetables, however this will not infuse the vegetables with the flavour of the wood smoke). The right time to cook the vegetables is when you have a good bed of hot coals covering the whole surface of the fire. The aubergine will take the longest to cook and you will need the fire to last until the aubergine is well cooked.

Peel the aubergine and slice into 6-8 mm thin slices along the length. Cut each capsicum in half and remove the core and seeds. Roast the aubergine and capsicum over an open grill on a wood fire. The wood fire should be at the stage of smoky hot glowing coals emitting small flames. Both the aubergine and capsicum will wilt when properly cooked.

The capsicum skin will burn and the aubergine will also roast to a brown colour with patches of black. This is okay as long as it does not burn dry. Remove and let cool; clean away all the burnt outside skin. Slice the capsicum and aubergine into long thin sections and toss together in a large bowl.

Prepare the dressing by crushing the salt and garlic into a paste and mix with the fresh lemon juice and extra virgin olive oil. Bring all the ingredients into a large bowl and mix well, coating all the vegetables with the salt, garlic, lemon juice and oil. Add the black pepper, oregano and caraway seeds and transfer into a decorative bowl ready to serve.

This salad keeps well refrigerated in a sealed glass or plastic container and makes a great filling for wraps to take to work or to have as a light dinner. I have used the leftovers the next day with cold ham, lettuce, tomato or leftover barbecued lamb wrapped in Lebanese bread. Serves 4-6 people.

Broad bean salad

Ingredients

1½ cups dried broad beans, soaked overnight until softened ready to cook

40 ml lemon juice

½ teaspoon garlic paste

½ level teaspoon salt (1.5 g)

40 ml extra virgin olive oil

½ cup chopped parsley (15 g)

Legume salads are popular in Lebanese food and this recipe can be made using various types of legumes. You can substitute the broad beans used here for chickpeas, red kidney beans or a combination of any of the three using the same salad dressing .

See the section on preparing legumes in the 'Basic ingredients' section at the front of the book. Cook the broad beans until they are well done. Allow to cool and place in a mixing bowl. Mix together the garlic paste, oil, lemon juice and parsley, dress the cold beans with the dressing and place in a salad bowl ready to serve. Serves 3-4 people.

Cauliflower salad

Ingredients

2 cups tahini dressing (see page 18)

4 cups cauliflower pieces (360 g)

This type of salad using the tahini dressing shown at the front of the book is another typical style of salad where you can substitute one ingredient for another. This salad can also be made using the cooked stalks from silverbeat instead of cauliflower. Trim away the green leaf section, lightly boil and toss in with the dressing.

To make the cauliflower salad cut off two cups (or trees as I call them) from a head of the cauliflower. Trim off any excess stalks and lightly steam or boil. Cook the pieces so that they are just right and still crunchy. Let cool and toss in a bowl with the tahini dressing. Garnish with some chopped parsley. Serves 3-4 people.

Dips and spreads

Babba ghannouj

2 medium sized aubergines (1.3 kg)

1½ tablespoons tahini (23 g)

1 level teaspoon garlic paste (7 g)

80 ml fresh lemon juice

This dip is the one everybody asks me to make every time I have a dinner party. I have been told that it is the best they have ever tasted and the secret to this is in the cooking of the aubergine. Roasting the aubergine on an open wood fire gives the dip a smoky flavour that you would not normally achieve using a conventional oven. If you do not have a wood fire you can still make the dip by baking the aubergine in an oven and it will taste delicious but without the fabulous smoky flavour.

To make Babba ghannouj, slow cook the aubergines over a smoky wood fire until it is charred and soft. Do not cook over a fire that is too hot as it will burn and become dry. Once cooked let them cool and peel away the charred skin and remove the soft cooked flesh into a mixing bowl. Mix in the garlic, most of the lemon juice and crush the flesh with a fork as you mix the ingredients together. Crush the ingredients into an even consistency breaking the large lumps of cooked flesh to form a lumpy paste. Add the tahini and keep mixing. At this stage you can do a taste test to establish if it is needs more lemon or tahini. The dip should be a balance of flavours between the smoky aubergine flesh, the tahini, the lemon juice and the garlic. If you need more lemon juice or tahini add some, but be careful not to add too much. The tahini and lemon juice can become overpowering if you add too much to the mixture.

Once you have made the dip, decant into a bowl. Serve slightly chilled or at room temperature as a starter or alongside barbecued meat. To present this dip in a spectacular way, you can hollow out half an aubergine and use the shell as the bowl. Sprinkle the top with a little paprika and garnish with a mint or parsley sprig. You can also drizzle a little good quality virgin olive oil over the top.

This dip is traditionally eaten with flat Lebanese bread, cut or torn into wedges or baked in an oven and cracked into corn chip sizes. Alternatively you can use Italian style crusty bread, plain corn chips or vegetable sticks such as carrots or celery or served alongside a meal. Serves 3-4 people.

Hummus

Ingredients

1 1/2 cups dried chickpeas (250 g)

1½ tablespoons tahini (22 g)

1 teaspoon garlic paste (7 g)

80 ml fresh lemon juice

Cook the dry chickpeas in a pot of boiling water until they are soft (see page 10). When they are well cooked you should be able to squeeze a chickpea between your fingers, crushing it into a smooth paste. While the chickpeas are still hot, drain and keep the water. Blend the chickpeas to a smooth paste using an electric blender. Add some of the drained water back to the paste to get the right thickness, creating a smooth paste. Then add to the blender the garlic, tahini and two thirds of the lemon juice leaving a little to add later. You may add a little more water if it is too thick. Give the mixture another blend to mix all the ingredients, then decant into a mixing bowl. Taste the hummus to see if it needs some more lemon juice or tahini and adjust to taste. Give the dip another stir and serve in a dipping bowl with some Lebanese bread, crackers or plain corn chips. You can decorate the dip with cooked chickpeas, a sprinkle of paprika and a drizzle of virgin olive oil.

Chilli dipping sauce

Ingredients

10 orange habanero chillies (30 g)

2 large tomatoes (260 g)

2 medium red capsicums (400 g)

1 peeled brown onion (130 g)

1 teaspoon rock salt (8 g)

80 ml white vinegar

2 large tablespoons tomato paste (60 g)

Chillies are one of my passions, and making chilli sauce is great fun. There are so many varieties of hot and sweet chillies and peppers with which to experiment, and many different bases to use. This one is a simple but very tasty tomato-based chilli sauce. If you like hot food you will find this very addictive - so be careful you may get hooked.

For this chilli sauce you can use any variety of red chillies and make it as strong or as mild as you like by altering the ratio of capsicum, tomato and chillies. I like to use habanero chillies because they are very hot as well as having a distinctive flavour.

Prepare the ingredients by peeling and cutting the onion in half, cut the capsicums in halves and remove the core and take out the eyes from the tomatoes and pull the stalks off the chillies. Place the above ingredients in a saucepan and just cover with water, bring to a simmer and cook for half an hour. Drain and let cool keeping the water in a container to use later. This water is full of flavour and heat and can be used as stock.

In a blender add the cooled ingredients, together with the rock salt, vinegar and tomato paste, add some of the leftover water and blend into a runny sauce. Return to the saucepan and bring to a simmer reducing to a thick dipping sauce. You can add more of the left over water extending the cooking time and reduce the sauce again. For a richer sauce, add more tomato paste and more water and simmer some more until it is rich and thick. This sauce is excellent with lamb kebabs and wood fire baked potato.

Zahtar

Ingredients

10 g dry oregano

28 g sesame seeds

15 g sumac

100 ml extra virgin olive oil

This is a herbaceous tangy dip which is eaten with Lebanese bread. It is an elegant and quick dip to prepare. Simply mix all the ingredients together and it is ready to serve. Serve in a decorative bowl with some Lebanese flat bread or an Italian crusty white loaf. Alternatively, you can serve the mixture dry, with the olive oil in a separate side dish: that way you dip your bread into the oil and then into the dry mix.

Savoury pastries

Sambousek

Ingredients

3¼ cups plain flour (500 g)

200 g ghee

100 ml cup olive oil (½ cup)

1 teaspoon salt (8 g)

1 cup water

300 g of pine nut mix (see page 15)

Grape seed oil for frying (olive oil optional)

These pine nut mix filled pastries are absolutely deliciously morish, making a great addition to a mezza dinner party. I always serve something to dip them into, like a chilli sauce, hummus or even a yoghurt dip. They take a little time to make but it is worth it when you taste them.

To make the pine nut mix please refer to 'The basics'. section at the front of the book. Begin by mixing the flour, oil and ghee together and knead. Gradually add the water until the dough is elastic and smooth. This type of dough is very different to bread dough and will feel oily and silky, not sticky like normal bread dough. The ghee and oil will help the dough fry quickly and become crispy.

Once you have made the dough, roll out into a flat sheet using a rolling pin. Roll the dough not too thin or too thick, but thick enough so that it will hold together firmly. Using a round dough cutter between 8-9 cm in diameter, cut the sheet into round discs. Using a basting brush wet the outer edge of one of the discs with a little milk and place enough pine nut mix on one side, allowing you to fold the other side

over creating a half moon shape. Using a fork, press around the other edge sealing the parcel. This is a simple and quick way of sealing the parcel or you can be more creative by pinching and rolling the edge. Do the same for all the other discs, then collect the leftover dough and knead into a ball and repeat the procedure until you have used all the dough.

I prefer to use grape seed oil for deep frying as it is a hotter oil than most oils and crisps quickly. Remember you only need to cook the pastry as the inside has been precooked. Place 500-700 ml of oil into a deep pan and heat until very hot. The number of parcels you cook at once depends on the size of your pan. Just be careful not to crowd the oil with too many parcels. This will lower the temperature of the oil and will not crisp the dough quickly. Keep turning the parcels over and you will find they will brown quickly. Cook until golden brown, remove and place in a bowl ready to serve hot and crispy. Serves 3-4 people.

Manoush

Ingredients

500 g basic dough or pizza dough (see page 16)

1 cup zahtar dip (See Dips and spreads)

1 cup chopped onion, optional (130 g)

The following two recipes use the same dough to form the base for their different toppings. My mother would often make both at the same time. The Manoush was eaten in the morning, hot straight out of the oven for breakfast. The Lahem ahjeen was cooked around lunchtime with a selection of other lunchtime food.

The topping for the Manoush is the Zahtar dip from the 'Dips and spreads' section earlier in the book. Once you have made the basic dough, divide into small flat round pizza bases the size of a small teacup saucer, around 12 cm in diameter. Create dimples on the surface by pushing your fingers into the dough and coat the base with the Zahtar mixture, making sure it is even and fills the dimples. Sprinkle the optional chopped onion on top, along with a little extra olive oil and bake in a preheated oven until the dough rises and the edges are golden brown.

Serves 3-4 people.

Lahem ahjeen

Ingredients

500 g basic dough or pizza dough (see page 16)

1¼ cup coarse minced lamb (250 g)

2 cups chopped onion (260 g)

2 cups chopped tomato (320 g)

1 level teaspoon white pepper (3 g)

1 level teaspoon allspice (3 g)

1 level teaspoon crushed rock salt (3 g)

In a bowl bring together and mix the coarse minced lamb, chopped onion, tomato and spices. Repeat the same method for the bases as with the Manoush. Top each base with a good covering of the meat mix and bake in a preheated oven until the dough rises and the edges are golden brown. Serves 3-4 people.

Fatayer

Ingredients

500 g plain flour

150 ml water (¾ cup)

150 ml extra virgin olive oil (¾ cup)

1 teaspoon salt (3 g)

1 teaspoon cracked pepper (3 g)

250 g chopped fresh silverbeet

2 finely chopped onions (260 g)

2 finely chopped tomatoes (260 g)

1 lemon

These pyramid-shaped vegetarian parcels are very tasty and healthy. This recipe uses a similar dough to that used in Sambousek but without the ghee. Traditionally made using silverbeet, onion and tomato, but you can experiment by adding to the mixture a variety of extras, such as chopped black olives and fetta cheese. Wholemeal instead of white flour can also be used for a healthier option.

Bring all the chopped silverbeet, tomato and onion into a bowl, then season with cracked pepper, squeeze half a lemon over the top and mix well. If you are adding extra ingredients make sure not to add too much and overpower the main ingredients. For fetta cheese, I would add around 40 to 50 grams and around 20 to 30 grams of chopped black olives.

In a bowl add the flour, salt, olive oil and mix as you slowly add water. Knead the mix until it is smooth and silky. This type of dough should be elastic and smooth, similar to the dough used in Sambousek. Once the dough is ready, roll out in a thin sheet around 1 to 2 mm thick using a rolling pin. The sheet will need to be thick enough so that it holds its shape when it is folded. Cut the sheet into 14 cm squares and with a basting brush wet the outer perimeter with milk. Place some of the mix in the middle of the square, enough so that you can pull up the four corners to a point enclosing the filling. Squeeze the sides of the pyramid sealing the edges. Repeat the filling process for each square and use the remaining dough to make more squares. If you have some filling left over you can us this to make a delicious omelette, just mix in enough eggs and fry in a non-stick pan.

Grease and flour an oven pan and bake the pyramid parcels at 180 to 200 degrees Celsius in a preheated oven until the parcels have golden brown peaks. A good idea for something different is to add fetta cheese and green olives to half the mixture and make half with and half without. A temptingly delicious Fatayer can be eaten hot or cold and goes well with the other pastry dishes. Serves 3-4 people.

Cooking with lamb

Kebbe

Ingredients

4½ cups mutton mince (500 g)

300 g pine nut mix (see page 15)

600 g cracked wheat

2 large onions (360 g)

2 teaspoons white pepper (6 g)

2 teaspoons allspice (6 g)

2 teaspoons cinnamon (6 g)

1 level teaspoon ground rock salt (3 g)

Soak the cracked wheat in warm water until soft (1-2 minutes), drain and squeeze dry. Mince the large onion using a meat grinder or food processor. Then mix the soaked cracked wheat, minced mutton, onion and spices in a large bowl making sure the spices and onion are evenly distributed.

This recipe makes 12 to 15 balls or can be made as a tray of Kebbe. To make a tray of Kebbe oil a baking pan or shallow casserole dish using olive oil. Spread one half of the main mix in the oiled pan creating a base layer around 2.5 cm thick and then spread the pine nut mixture over the top. Cover the first layer and pine nut mixture with the remaining mince creating a top layer with the same 2.5 cm thickness. Score a cross hatch pattern over the top and drizzle with olive oil. You can do the same in small ramekins for single serves.

To make the recipe into Kebbe balls, place a small amount of mixture equivalent to the size of an egg, in the palm of one hand and hollow out with your other hand. Place the finger of your free hand down through the middle of the ball and rotate the meat with your other hand while pressing down with your finger to create a cavity. Fill the cup shape with mixture, close into a football shape with a slight point on each end.

The Kebbe in the tray and ramekins are cooked in a fan forced oven at around 220 degrees Celsius for around 45 minutes. The balls are best deep fried until golden brown using either olive or grape seed oil (which is a much hotter oil and browns more quickly). When cooked, serve the balls, ramekins or slices from the tray with fresh home-made natural yoghurt, or yoghurt sauce, and one of the salads of your choice from the 'Fresh salad' section. Serves 3-4 people.

Red kidney beans and lamb

Ingredients

400 g lamb backstraps cut into eight equal
sections (mutton makes an excellent
substitute for more flavour)

200 g soaked red kidney beans
(or 800 g tinned beans drained)

1 medium onion (130 g chopped)

2 cloves chopped garlic (10 g)

2 tablespoons concentrated tomato paste (70 g)

1 level teaspoon allspice (3 g)

1 level teaspoon cinnamon (3 g)

1 level teaspoon ground white pepper (3 g)

1 level teaspoon ground rock salt (3 g)

Soak the beans in water for 24 hours, changing
the water after the first 12 hours (use 1 teaspoon of
baking powder in the first soak).

Cut the lamb into equal chunks and in a large
saucepan seal with olive oil. Add to the saucepan
the garlic and onion and cook until the onions are
sautéed. Then add the spices, beans and 2 litres
of water to the mix. Bring to a simmer then add the
tomato paste. Stir occasionally while simmering with
the pot lid ¾ closed. Depending how dry or fresh your
beans are will determine how much extra water you
will need to add and how long you will need to cook
the beans and lamb. It may take up to a little over an
hour to cook the soaked beans until they are soft.

As the ingredients reduce, add more water until the
beans are tender (pinch a bean to test if it is soft).
When the beans are well cooked the sauce should
be thick and rich and the lamb falling apart. If you are
using tinned beans, add the washed tinned beans
approximately 15-20 minutes before the meat is
tender and the sauce has reduced. This dish freezes
and reheats well. Serves 4-6 people.

Green beans
and lamb

Ingredients

400 g cubed lamb

4 cups fresh green beans chopped to
6 cm lengths (400 g)

1 large onion (130 g chopped)

2 large tablespoons of
concentrated tomato paste (70 g)

1 level teaspoon allspice (3 g)

1 level teaspoon cinnamon (3 g)

1 level teaspoon white pepper (3 g)

1 level teaspoon ground rock salt (3 g)

2 cloves chopped garlic (10 g)

In a large deep saucepan with olive oil sauté the onions and chopped garlic then add the cubed lamb and spices. Cook for 1-2 minutes, sealing the lamb. Add 4 cups of water and the tomato paste and stir whilst bringing to a simmer. Cook for 1-1½ hours until the lamb is tender. A good hint is to leave the saucepan lid ¾ closed as this will help in the reduction. The liquid should reduce into a thick and rich sauce. Add a half cup of water, the green beans and cook for a further 10-15 minutes reducing the sauce once again. Serve with freshly made 'Lebanese rice' (see page 16).

This recipe can be made without meat as shown in the 'Healthy vegetarian' section of the book (see page 104). Take the time to look for the best and freshest green beans you can find as this will greatly contribute to the quality of the meal. Also use a tender cut of lamb, such as leg, shoulder or backstraps. Serves 4-6 people.

Stuffed marrow, *Kousa*

Ingredients

8 green marrow (1.3 kg)

2 cups long grain rice (400 g)

2 cups coarse ground lamb (400 g)

3-4 lamb chops

1 level teaspoon white pepper (3 g)

1 level teaspoon rock salt (3 g)

1 level teaspoon allspice (3 g)

4 large tablespoons concentrated
tomato paste (130 g)

4 ½ cups of water

This is a hearty filling winter dish. My mother would make this dish alongside rolled grape vine leaves in the same pot. Similar to the vine leaves recipe, it is made using the same lamb rice stuffing, tomato base and lamb chops placed at the bottom of the pot.

The marrow should have a base around 5-6 cm in diameter and should have an overall length of around 16-20 cm. Using a corer, hollow out each marrow leaving a wall thickness of around 3-5 mm. Be careful not to punch a hole through the base or make the base too thin. Put aside while making the stuffing.

In a bowl mix together the ground lamb, rice and spices. Stuff the hollowed out marrow with the rice mixture leaving around 2.5 cm from the top. Oil a deep pot with olive oil and lay the lamb chops at the bottom. Carefully arrange the stuffed marrow over the chops. Mix the tomato paste in 4 ½ cups of water and pour over the marrow. Put the pot on a low heat and cook for 30-45 minutes, checking every 10 minutes that the pot is not too dry. When cooked the rice should look puffy and the filling expanded to fill the marrow. Best served hot and fresh. Serves 4-6 people.

Lamb backstraps

Ingredients

600 g lamb back straps

1 medium onion (130 g chopped)

1 large tablespoon concentrated
tomato paste (35 g)

3 well ripened, peeled and chopped
tomatoes (400 g)

1 level teaspoon allspice (3 g)

1 level teaspoon cinnamon (3 g)

1 level teaspoon white pepper (3 g)

1 level teaspoon ground rock salt (3 g)

4 garlic cloves sliced into long sections (20 g)

2-3 large potatoes (250 g peeled)

2 litres grape seed or olive oil

Cut potatoes into wedges. Deep fry the potato wedges in a high temperature oil such as grape seed oil until a golden brown colour. Strain and leave aside. Chop the tomatoes into small sections and place aside. Cut the lamb backstraps into 10 cm sections and put aside. Mix all the spices in a mixing bowl and add the meat, making sure to coat all sides of the lamb sections. Pierce the meat sections with a small paring knife and stuff with a good slice of garlic.

In a deep saucepan heat 2-3 tablespoons of olive oil and seal the seasoned meat. Add to the onions to the pot and sauté, then add 4 cups of water, the remaining spices, the tomato paste, the chopped tomatoes and allow to simmer until the sauce is thick and rich and the meat becomes tender and flaky. Add the cooked wedges to the pot and continue cooking for another 15 minutes. Serve with 'Lebanese rice' (see page 16), fresh bought Lebanese flat bread and a good cabernet sauvignon for warm winter dinners to remember. This dish freezes and reheats well.
Serves 4-6 people.

Rolled grapevine leaves

Ingredients

300 g fresh grapevine leaves

(frozen or jarred variety if fresh is not available)

2 cups long grain rice (400 g)

2 cups coarse ground lamb (400 g)

3-4 lamb chops

1 level teaspoon white pepper (3 g)

1 level teaspoon rock salt (3 g)

1 level teaspoon allspice (3 g)

4 large tablespoons concentrated

tomato paste (130 g)

4 $^1/_2$ cups of water

This dish is similar to Stuffed marrow (Kousa) as it uses the same type of stuffing and you can cook both in the same pot. The two complement each other and make a hearty main meal.

Mix the lamb, rice and spices in a bowl. If you are picking the leaves from a grapevine, pick the ones that are the softest and are not too small. If you do not have fresh vine leaves you can buy the pickled variety from a Lebanese, or Greek delicatessen.

Lay the grapevine leaf down flat with the shiny side facing down and place some of the rice mixture in a row near the stem. Roll in the outer edges and roll the leaf toward you forming a cylinder. This is similar to rolling spring rolls. Adjust the amount of rice stuffing according to the size of the vine leaf making sure that the rolls are tight but not overstuffed. If they are overstuffed they will break when the rice expands. When you have rolled the first leaf lay it over the lamb chops nesting each one after the other, side by side, into a layer working up to the top of the pot. Mix the tomato paste with 4 $^1/_2$ cups of water and pour over the rolled vine leaves. Place the pot on a slow heat

and cook for 30-40 minutes, checking that it is not too dry. Break one of the vine leaves to check if the rice is cooked. If it is too dry and still firm add a little more water and cook until the rice is tender.

When you are cooking the two recipes together, 'Rolled grapevine leaves' and 'Stuffed marrow', there is no real preference of how to stack them in the pot. As long as they are done carefully you can stack them side by side or on top of each other. I have found the method that works for me is the side by side, having marrow one side and grapevine leaves on the other. This allows easy access to both.

The aroma of this food is wonderfully inviting. The chops at the bottom really give the dish a great lamb flavour, and the fresh vine leaves add a lovely tang. This should be served with fresh Lebanese flat bread and a good quality red wine.

Serves 4-6 people.

Okra and lamb

Ingredients

400 g cubed lamb or mutton

240 g fresh green okra beans

1 heaped tablespoon coriander seeds (8 g)

Fresh chopped coriander (8 g)

1 level teaspoon allspice (3 g)

1 level teaspoon cinnamon (3 g)

1 level teaspoon white pepper (3 g)

1 level teaspoon rock salt (3 g)

3 cloves garlic (15 g)

80 ml fresh lemon juice

(or 40 ml pure pomegranate concentrated syrup)

1½ cups chopped onions (195 g)

2 large tablespoons tomato paste (70 g)

This is a fabulous dish that bursts with flavours of lamb, coriander, garlic, pomegranate and traditional middle eastern spices. Cooked to perfection the lamb melts in your mouth.

Deep fry the okra bean in olive oil until dark brown. Strain the cooked okra bean from the oil and set it aside. In a deep pan sauté the onions in olive oil and add the lamb, turning to seal the surface of the meat and then reduce the heat. While the meat is cooking, in a mortar and pestle crush the rock salt, coriander seed and garlic into a coarse paste. Add the white pepper, fresh coriander and the crushed spices to the meat and cook for 1 minute. Add 6 cups of water and simmer on a low heat. Then add the tomato paste, lemon juice or pomegranate syrup and simmer for at least 45 minutes, checking on the sauce to make sure it reduces into a thick, rich consistency. Add the okra bean and cook for another 15 minutes. You may need to add a little water to cook the meat until it becomes tender. When ready, serve with fresh Lebanese rice (see page 16) and fresh Lebanese bread. A personal favourite of mine, unforgettable! Serves 4-6 people.

Aubergines stuffed with lamb

Ingredients

400 g lamb and pine nut mixture (see page 15)

8 lady finger aubergines around 20-25 cm long

(These are the thin long continental aubergines.)

3 tablespoons concentrated tomato paste (90 g)

My mother would always have some of the pine nut mix in the freezer as this made the preparation even simpler. This recipe can be cooked by stacking the aubergines in a pot or lining them up in a flat casserole dish. I prefer to line the aubergine face up, side by side in a casserole dish and bake them in an oven. The aubergines you will need are the long thin variety. When selecting make sure they are not too thin but have a round base around 4-5 cm. This is so you have enough room to stuff the pine nut mix into the aubergines. You will need 8-10 depending on the size of your pot or casserole dish.

Peel each aubergine and cut off the head. Make a deep incision along the length of the vegetable but do not cut through to the other side. Push your finger into the incision pushing the flesh apart and leaving a cavity. Fill the cavity with the pine nut mixture. Oil the casserole dish and place the aubergines in the dish side by side. Mix the tomato paste into 3 cups of water and pour around the aubergine, letting the mixture flow in between. Cover the casserole dish with aluminium foil and bake for 45-50 minutes at 180 degrees Celsius. Remove the aluminium foil after

30 minutes and check the cooking process, if it is too dry add some water and cook for the remaining time. When cooked, the aubergine flesh should be soft and floating in a thick tomato sauce. This is a hearty, warming winter dish traditionally served with hot Lebanese rice (see page 16), fresh Lebanese bread and of course, a good full-bodied dry red wine. Serves 4-6 people.

Lamb and red wine sausages

Ingredients

500 g beef mince

500 g mutton mince

500 g pork mince

300 g minced pork fat

30 g crushed coriander seeds

10 g ground white pepper

10 g ground black pepper

10 g ground pimento (allspice)

10 g ground rock or sea salt

1 packet cleaned and salted
natural sausage skins

Red merlot that you like to drink

This is a recipe for home-made, spiced, red wine sausages and requires some skill and equipment. You may be able to buy the ground meats and the sausage skins from a good quality butcher or make your own mince at home. Do not buy lean mince or meat as you will need the fat content to keep the sausages moist. Using a good quality food processor such as a, Kenwood Chef, or Kitchen Aid, you can use the sausage-making attachment to make the sausages. Otherwise, you can use a cast iron hand-cranked meat grinder with similar attachments.

Mince the meats if you are making your own, and mix together, including the ground pork fat and spices in a large glass or stainless steel bowl. Using a good quality merlot, pour enough wine to cover the meat and mix through. Cover with cling wrap and refrigerate for 24 hours. After marinating, the meat mixture is ready to be turned into sausages.

The next step is to set up the equipment using a nozzle around 1.5 cm in diameter. Feed one of the sausage skins onto the long nozzle at the end of the attachment: these skins are several metres long.

Start the machine and feed the mince through until it starts extruding into the sausage skin. With one hand on the nozzle slowly release the skin on the nozzle as the meat extrudes and with the other hand support the sausage as it fills, ensuring that it is an even diameter with no bumps or twists. Extrude around half a metre and then twist the filled section into individual sausages of around 10 cm in length. Repeat the process until the skin is finished then reload another section of skin to repeat the process.

When you have completed and used all the meat mixture you will need to firm up the sausages by hanging them in your refrigerator. Place a tray under the sausages to catch any dripping red wine and juices. Leave them to hang for 24 hours. Once they are firm you can cook these sausages as you would any other sausage and serve with other barbecued meats and salads. Makes around 1.5 kg of sausages.

Cooking with beef

Corned beef chilli sauce

Ingredients

800 g fresh corned beef minced (tinned optional)

2 large onions chopped (320 g)

4 heaped tablespoons tomato paste (120 g)

Chillies to taste, fresh or powdered,

1 teaspoon paprika (3 g)

1½ cups water (300 ml)

This is a Ghanaian recipe where you will need to make your own corned beef mince from a corned section of beef that you would normally buy from your butcher. To do this you can use either a cast iron, hand-operated mincer or an electric one. Do not use a food blender or processor as this will shred and tear the meat and produce the wrong texture.

Set the meat grinder up and cut the corned beef into long, thin sections. Start turning the handle as you drop the long sections into the feeder, one at a time as you grind. Once completed, set aside for later. Using plenty of oil in a deep saucepan, fry the onions until they are starting to brown and then add the corned mince and cook - stirring and crumbling the meat as it cooks. Then add the spices and chillies and cook for around 6-8 minutes, browning the meat. Add the water and tomato paste and reduce to a simmer and let cook for two hours until the meat is tender and the sauce has thickened to a rich consistency.

Once the corned beef mince sauce is cooked, you can serve with the 'Fermented corn dumplings' (see page 107). This is one of the two sauces you can use to serve with 'Fermented corn dumplings' and is my personal favourite. The other is the 'Chilli fish sauce' on page 118. You can try to make your own style of sauce to go with the flavour of the corn dumplings by experimenting with different vegetables and meats, such as chicken or pork.

Alternatively, this simply delicious sauce can be matched with other root or starch vegetables, such as boiled potato, yams, cassava, and taro. African food uses many starchy root vegetables boiled and mashed, served alongside spicy sauces made with red meat or fish. Depending on the region's agriculture and season these sauces could be beef, chicken, seafood or vegetable based.

If you do not want to make your own corned beef mince, a quick and easy solution is to use a tinned variety of corned beef. This is convenient but not near as nice and healthy. Whenever possible, I recommend the fresher alternative as it is so much better. Serves 6-8 people.

Ground nut soup

Ingredients

600 g stewing beef

2 large onions chopped (300 g)

2 peeled and crushed tomatoes (250 g)

½ cup smooth peanut paste (150 g)

2 large chillies (80 g)

2 teaspoons paprika (6 g)

1 teaspoon salt (3 g)

1 teaspoon white pepper (3 g)

This is a simple, traditional Ghanaian peanut soup which is served with a starchy dumpling or root vegetable. The soup can be made with any meat from chicken to mud crab, I personally prefer to use beef with these recipes. This can be made as spicy as you like by controlling how much chilli you add.

Begin by cutting the stewing beef into 3-4 cm chunks and season with the salt and pepper. In a deep pan, seal the meat and add the onions, cooking for a few minutes. Add 4 cups of water and cook for 1-1½ hours on a low simmering heat while constantly checking and topping up the water when needed.

Prepare the tomatoes by blanching and peeling, then crush by hand or in blender. After 1½ hours of cooking the beef, add the tomatoes to the pan. Cook for a further half hour and then add the chillies and half a cup of peanut paste. Cook for a further 1 hour on a low, simmering heat. Perform a taste test, and if it needed add more salt or chillies accordingly. The meat at this stage should be very tender and the flavours cooked right through. If the soup is too thick adjust with water and cook for a little longer. When it is ready it should be at a good consistency, with the meat very tender and flaky. Serves 6-8 people.

This recipe and the one for 'Palm soup' are similar in the way they are served, with a starchy dumpling or root vegetable 'Foo foo' (see page 68). Root vegetables such as cassava, taro, and yams can be purchased from Indian food stores that stock Fijian or Pacific island groceries.

Palm soup

Ingredients

600 g stewing beef

2 large onions chopped (300 g)

2 peeled and crushed tomatoes (250 g)

2 cups okra beans, chopped in halves (150 g)

1 cup diced eggplant (70 g)

1 cup red palm nut paste (200 g)

2 large chillies (80 g)

2 teaspoons paprika (6 g)

1 teaspoon salt (3 g)

1 teaspoon white pepper (3 g)

This recipe can also be made with beef, chicken, lamb, crab and seafood. For this you will need to visit an African grocer to purchase red palm nut paste or go online and have it sent to you. There is no other substitute for this unique flavour. This product is made from the cooked red palm nut, pounded into a paste, strained and canned.

Start by cutting the meat into large chunks, around 3-4 cm in size and season with salt and pepper. In a deep pan seal the meat using olive oil then add the onions and sauté for a few minutes. Add 4 cups of water followed by the chopped okra bean and diced eggplant. Bring to a simmer and cook for 60-90 minutes on a low heat. After 60-90 minutes remove the meat from the broth and set aside. Using a hand held blender or a bench blender, blend the soup and return to the pot. Then return the meat to the pot and bring to a simmer. The blended okra bean and eggplant will add flavour, thickness and depth to the soup. Now add the cup of palm paste, the chillies, the crushed tomatoes and cook for another 1½ hours. As it is cooking the fragrance will change as the flavours combine. Taste the soup to determine whether you need to add more salt, pepper, or chilli. This soup should be a thick, hearty rich consistency with the meat tender and flaky.

This soup can be served with starchy dumplings such as 'Foo foo' (see page 68) or boiled root vegetables such as cassava and potato. These types of root vegetables including cassava, taro, and yams can be purchased from Indian food stores that stock Fijian or Pacific island groceries.

To really capture the theme of African food, serve the food using dinnerware and a table setting that are African in style and colour. These saucy meat recipes freeze well and can be reheated and used later for meals. Serves 6-8 people.

Foo foo

Ingredients

3 medium size potatoes

1 packet of potato starch (250 g)

1 packet frozen cassava (alternative)

Traditionally the Ghanaian people would use a large wooden mortar and pestle to crush the root vegetable and make the dumpling. The mortar and pestle is so big that the pestle is used while standing up, with the mortar on the floor. One lady would pound the cassava while another, sitting next to the mortar, would turn the ingredients by hand after each stroke. They would do this rhythmically without missing a beat, singing as they work.

This is a simple way of making a starchy dumpling similar to the way Ghanaians make them. To start, peel and boil the potatoes, then drain and mash. Keep the mash in the pot as you will be working the mixture over the stove on a low heat. Add around half a cup of warm water and sprinkle 3 tablespoons of starch over the mash and mix quickly pulling the mixture from the middle to the side of the pot. Do this quickly while holding the pot firmly. Repeat this process until the mash has become silky and smooth, as if you were making bread dough.

When you have reached the silky, smooth firm dough stage, let the mixture cool. Using wet hands so that the dough does not stick to your fingers, separate the mixture into serving size balls and serve with the 'Palm' or 'Ground nut' soup (see page 64 and 67).

For an alternative to the starchy dumpling boil the frozen cassava until it is tender and cut into serving size portions, place in a bowl and serve alongside the soup. If you cannot find fresh cassava, a boiling potato such as Pink Eye or Desiree is just as delicious as a substitute. Serves 3-4 people.

Chicken

Chicken rice

Ingredients

1 kg chicken pieces (or selected cuts)

4 cups chicken stock (1 L)

2 cups long grain rice (400 g)

200 g coarse cut lamb

¼ cup pine nuts (40 g)

¼ cup blanched almonds (45 g)

1 level teaspoon white pepper (3 g)

1 level teaspoon rock salt (3 g)

40 ml olive oil

Cook the chicken in a big pot with enough water to make 4 cups of chicken stock. Drain the stock and let the cooked chicken cool. Then flake the chicken removing the white flesh leaving the bones behind. Keep the chicken flesh covered and warm as this will be added to the cooked rice.

In a deep saucepan brown the pine nuts and almonds in 20 ml olive oil, remove and place aside. The pine nuts will brown very quickly, so do these first and remove, then brown the almonds. Next remove the almonds and add the remaining olive oil and brown the coarse cut lamb.

Add the chicken stock, salt and pepper to the same large saucepan used to cook the coarse cut lamb, bring the stock to a simmer and then add the rice. Leave the lid of the saucepan just closing the top of the pot, leaving a gap to allow the steam to escape as you cook the rice. When the stock has almost evaporated take the saucepan off the heat, completely close the pot with the lid, and let sit for 10 minutes. This should finish the rice cooking in its own heat.

When the rice has rested for ten 10 minutes, remove from the pot into a very large serving dish and mix in most of the chicken meat, pine nuts and almonds. Garnish the top of the rice with the remaining pine nuts, almonds and chicken meat. Best served hot!

This is one of my favourite dishes and makes a great accompaniment to 'Char grilled lamb skewers' (see page 87) and 'Tabouleh' (see page 20). It can also be a meal on its own, served with a simple garden salad or fried vegetables. Serves 4-6 people.

Oven chicken pasta

Ingredients

1 kg chicken pieces of choice

2 onions sliced into rings (260 g)

1 pack of dry spaghetti (500 g)

2 large tablespoons concentrated tomato paste (70 g)

1 level teaspoon white pepper (3 g)

1 level teaspoon rock salt (3 g)

Place the chicken pieces in an oiled, shallow oven pan or large casserole dish. Sprinkle the onions and spices around and over the chicken pieces. Place in the oven and bake at 220 degrees Celsius until the chicken is almost cooked.

While the chicken is cooking boil the pasta with a little salt until just firm, just before al dente, then strain and put aside. Mix the tomato paste in to 3 cups of water and put aside, ready to use. When the chicken is almost cooked, mix in the pasta with the chicken pieces then pour the tomato paste over and mix in, coating everything in the pan. Put back in the oven and bake for 15 minutes turning over the chicken pieces and stirring the pasta. Add more tomato paste mixture or water if you need to make the dish more moist and saucier, as the pasta will tend to soak up the juices. Serves 4-6 people.

Jollof rice

Ingredients

500 g chicken fillet

1 litre chicken stock (4 cups)

2 large onions chopped (300 g)

2 peeled and crushed tomatoes (250 g)

4 cloves garlic (20g)

Green beans chopped (80 g)

Carrot chopped (80 g)

Celery chopped (80 g)

Capsicum chopped (80 g)

2 large chillies (80 g)

2 teaspoons paprika (6 g)

1 teaspoon salt (3 g)

1 teaspoon white pepper (3 g)

1 tablespoon fish sauce

2 cups white rice (400 g)

2 tablespoons of olive oil

Red palm nut oil (alternative)

2 tablespoons red palm nut paste (70 g alternative)

Jollof rice is a very popular Ghanaian recipe. Many different West African countries claim to be the creator of this delicious recipe. This style of cooking can be seen all over the world with such variations as Jambalaya and Paella. This could be accredited to the migration of people from Africa to Europe and the Americas. Whatever its history, it is an exciting and delicious recipe which is open to many variations. It can be made using different meats and vegetables that are in season at the time of cooking.

Begin by cutting the chicken fillet into small bite-sized chunks and season with the salt and pepper. Heat the chicken stock in a pot until simmering. Fry the chicken in the olive oil in a separate pan until lightly brown and remove from the pan and into the stockpot. An alternative, is to use red palm nut oil to fry the chicken and add 2 large tablespoons of red palm nut paste and stir into the chicken This will really give it a West African flavour. In the same pan add a little more olive oil and fry the onions, chillies, paprika and garlic, cooking for one minute then stirring in the fish sauce. Cook for another minute, then add the peeled and crushed tomatoes. Pour half the stock from the pot into the pan and then cook for 4-5 minutes at a simmer. Pour all the contents of the pan into the stockpot with the chicken. Bring to a simmer and stir in the rice. At this stage you can add the vegetables, which will become well cooked, together with the rice, or if you like your vegetables a little firm and crunchy, wait until the rice is almost cooked and then stir them in. A tip for cooking rice using the absorption method is to remove the pot from the heat just before the stock is totally absorbed by the rice. The remaining heat in the rice will finish the cooking process. Make sure your have used a 2:1 ratio of stock to rice so that it cooks right through. If the rice is too dry you can make it saucier by adding another half a cup of stock at the stage when you bring all the contents together.

This recipe can be made using beef, pork, lamb, prawns and different types of vegetables that are in season. Once cooked, serve the Jollof rice with salad, boiled eggs on the side and garnish with parsley or coriander. Serves 4-6 people.

Cooking with yoghurt

Kebbe in yoghurt

Ingredients

400 g minced lamb

300 g cracked wheat

2 large onions (360 g)

1 large raw egg (65 g)

600 ml natural set yoghurt (3 cups)

2 cloves garlic (10 g)

½ cup fresh chopped coriander leaf (15 g)

1½ teaspoons white pepper (4.5 g)

1½ teaspoons allspice (4.5 g)

½ teaspoon cinnamon (4.5 g)

1 level teaspoon ground rock salt (3 g)

This is a perfect hot dish for winter. It combines Kebbe balls with a yoghurt spiced with coriander and garlic. The recipe is a little complicated in the method and requires attention to detail especially while cooking.

This is the same as making normal Kebbe but without the stuffing. Soak the cracked wheat in warm water until soft (30 to 60 seconds) drain and squeeze dry. Mince the large onions using a meat grinder or a blender. If using a blender make sure that the onions are blended well and the mixture is smooth without large pieces. Next, mix the soaked cracked wheat, minced mutton, ground onion and spices in a large bowl. Mix well using your hands so the spices are evenly distributed.

Place a small amount of mixture equivalent to the size of an egg, in the palm of one hand and hollow it out with your other hand. Place the finger of your free hand down through the middle of the ball and rotate the meat with your other hand while pressing down with your finger to create a cavity. Close the cavity once you have made the ball. When you have finished, put the meatballs aside. Pour the 600 ml of yoghurt into a large saucepan and thin out with one or two cups of water. Break the raw egg into the yoghurt and whisk in well. Put the saucepan on a slow heat and bring to a simmer while constantly stirring (you must not stop stirring or the mixture will curdle). The texture at this stage should be like fresh cream, thick but runny, if it is too thick add some more water. Stir and bring back to a simmer and then add the kebbe balls. Cook for half an hour on a low heat checking the that the yoghurt does not reduce too much or stick to the bottom of the pan.

While the yoghurt and kebbe is cooking, in a mortar and pestle crush the garlic and coriander into a coarse paste. Lightly fry the garlic and coriander in a frying pan using two tablespoons of olive oil. Add the cooked garlic and coriander to the kebbe and yoghurt 15 minutes before the end of the cooking time to allow their flavours to simmer into the mixture.

When the cooking is done, the yoghurt should still be creamy, thick and saucy - like a good gravy - and not thick like a custard. Serves 4-6 people.

Cracked wheat with yoghurt

Ingredients

400 g cubed lamb fillet

2 cups coarse cracked wheat (260 g)

1 large onion cut into quarters (260 g)

2 litres vegetable stock or water (10 cups)

250 g cooked chickpeas

(or a 420g tin, drained)

1 level teaspoon white pepper (3 g)

1 level teaspoon rock salt (3 g)

Natural set yoghurt for topping

Red chillies (mild or hot)

This is a rustic dish which is very filling and very healthy. It combines the nutty flavour of cracked wheat with the fresh sharp tang of yoghurt. It is simple to make but very tasty. You can experiment with the recipe by using different types of stock such as beef or lamb instead of vegetable.

In a deep saucepan seal the lamb with olive oil and add 1½ litres of stock and cook the lamb until tender and flaky. This may take up to an hour or more. As the stock reduces, top up the saucepan with water or more stock so that you still have around the same volume of stock used at the start.

In a separate pan sauté the onions and add to the saucepan with the stock and lamb and then simmer for 2 minutes. Wash the cracked wheat and add to the saucepan with the stock, then add the cooked chickpeas. The cracked wheat will start cooking immediately and will absorb the stock and flavour. Reduce the heat to a simmer and cook for around 15 minutes. Keep an eye on the cracked wheat so that it does not become too dry. When the cracked wheat has absorbed most of the moisture and is similar in consistency to a risotto, remove from the heat and put aside to rest with the pan lid on. The remaining heat in the pot will finish the cooking process.

Serve on a flat plate with a topping of yoghurt and a garnish of sliced chillies or cucumber. The cracked wheat should be firm but well cooked, like the chickpeas, while the lamb should be tender and flaky. Serves 4-6 people.

Dumplings in yoghurt,

Shish Barak

Ingredients

minced lamb (200 g)

1 medium onion finely chopped (130 g)

2 cups white plain flour (320 g)

2-3 cups water (600 ml)

500 ml natural set yoghurt

1 raw egg (65 g)

1 cup chopped coriander leaf (30 g)

2 cloves garlic finely chopped (10 g)

butter (30 g)

1 level teaspoon white pepper (3 g)

2 level teaspoons ground rock salt (6 g)

This is my mother's favourite yoghurt dish. This recipe combines lamb filled dumplings cooked in a yoghurt sauce spiced with coriander and garlic. This delightful dish can be served hot or cold.

Mix into the lamb mince half the salt, white pepper and finely chopped onion and put aside. To make the dough mix the flour, 1 teaspoon of salt, water and knead well until the dough is shiny and elastic, but not too dry. Use a pasta machine if you have one, or a rolling pin to roll the dough to around one 1 mm thick or near enough as if you were making flat pasta.

Once you have rolled out the dough, cut out small discs from the flat sheet using a cookie cutter 3 to 5 cm in diameter. I use the top of a champagne flute which is the right size for making the small dumplings. Collect the remaining dough and bind together and roll out again to cut out more discs. Once you have used up all the dough to make the discs, you can start filling the dumplings.

To make a dumpling, pick up one disc and place a small amount of the meat mixture in the centre and fold the disc into a half moon shape sealing the outer rim. Then bring the two outer points together and pinch. Repeat the process using up all the punched out discs and the meat filling.

In a deep saucepan add 500 ml of naturally set yoghurt and thin out with 1½ cups of water. Whisk the egg into the yoghurt mixture until smooth. Put on a low heat and slowly bring to a slow simmer, always mixing and whisking. If it goes lumpy the heat was too high and you will need to start again. The sauce should be a like a smooth white custard. Slowly place the dumpling into the sauce and cook on a low heat so that the sauce and dumplings do not stick. Cook for 5-6 minutes and taste to see if the dumplings are cooked. Cook longer if needed.

In a small frying pan melt the butter and mix in the garlic and coriander and quickly cook for around 30 to 60 seconds. Pour the coriander and garlic over the dumplings and sauce, place the lid on and remove from the heat and let rest for 5 minutes. Just before serving, stir in the coriander and garlic dressing. Serves 4-6 people.

BBQ meats

Char grilled lamb skewers

Ingredients

500 g cubed lamb leg or backstraps

1 large onion, cut into eight sections (130 g)

1 capsicum optional,(200 g, cut into 8 or smaller sections)

8 cherry tomatoes

1 tablespoon garlic paste

1 level teaspoon allspice (3 g)

½ level teaspoon cinnamon (1.5 g)

1 level teaspoon white pepper (3 g)

1 level teaspoon crushed rock salt (3 g)

6-8 x 30 cm long metal skewers

Dice the lamb into 2.5-3 cm cubes or thereabouts. Place the diced lamb in a bowl and drizzle some olive oil over it to help the spices coat the meat. Mix in the garlic paste and spices then mix in the lamb, making sure that every piece of lamb is coated. Divide the meat evenly among the skewers. Begin to skewer the meat adding one vegetable piece in between the pieces of lamb. There is no particular order required as long as each skewer has one of each in succession. Cook on an open grill over a wood fire. The secret is to get the wood fire temperature right so that it char grills without burning the meat. Turn over the skewers constantly and cook medium rare.

To introduce a Ghanaian flavour into this dish, divide the meat into two piles before skewering. Mix in 2 or 3 large tablespoons of smooth or crunchy peanut butter and some chopped chillies into one pile and skewer. Skewer the other pile as described above and cook over the wood fire. Serves 6-8 people.

Char grilled garlic chicken skewers

Ingredients

500 g cubed chicken breast fillet, or

1 kg mixed chicken pieces

(use your preferred cuts)

1½ teaspoons garlic paste (10 g)

1 level teaspoon cracked pepper (4 g)

½ a lemon

8-10 x 30 cm long metal skewers

This is a great summer dish, quick and very easy to prepare for those languid, heat-filled days. It uses plenty of garlic and has a lovely smoky flavour created by cooking over an open wood fire. You can cook the chicken on skewers using the breast and thigh fillet, or you can use whole chicken pieces and barbecue over the grill.

To make the skewers, cut the chicken breast fillet into 1.5-2 cm cubes and coat with the garlic paste and cracked pepper. Squeeze the lemon over the pieces and mix well. If you have time you can marinate the chicken for a few hours in the fridge before you cook. This will infuse the lemon and garlic flavours right into the chicken. Divide the cubed chicken into equal portions and skewer onto the metal skewers ready to cook over an open fire or gas grill or BBQ. I always prefer to make my chicken skewers plain with no added vegetables, however, if you like you could add mushrooms, onions, even asparagus; it is up to your imagination. Experiment adding different vegetables that complement the flavour of the smoky spiced chicken.

To make the same recipe using whole chicken pieces select your favourite chicken pieces skin on or skin off. I prefer the skin on as it keeps the chicken moist, and I usually select the thigh Maryland and wing sections. Prepare the chicken using the same spices and lemon juice from half a lemon. Cook over a wood fire on an open grill.

This dish is well suited to go with the 'Oregano salad' (see page 24), 'Babba ghanoush' (see page 31) and fresh flat Lebanese bread. You can also serve a small side dish of dipping garlic paste or chilli sauce. Makes a great summertime weekend lunch, but the skewers are fantastic any time. The chicken can also be served cold. Serves 6-8 people.

Char grilled keftah

Ingredients

600 g minced lamb or mutton

2 onions (340 g)

2 cups chopped parsley (60 g)

1 level teaspoon cinnamon (3 g)

1 level teaspoon white pepper (3 g)

1 level teaspoon allspice (3 g)

1 level teaspoon crushed rock salt (3 g)

6-8 x 30 cm long metal skewers

For this recipe you can use lamb mince bought from a supermarket or butcher or you can make your own if you prefer. First peel and chop the onions into quarters and put aside. If you are making your own mince, set up your meat mincer and pass the onions, parsley and meat through. If you have bought minced lamb then just mince the onions and parsley.

Once you have minced your ingredients, mix together the minced meat, onions, parsley and spices in a bowl. Divide the mince mix into the amount of skewers you are making. On each skewer mould one of the divisions of the mince into a long sausage shape, similar to a normal thin sausage in length and thickness. Chill the prepared skewers in the refrigerator, this will help hold their shape when you are ready to cook them.

Char grill the skewers over a wood fire or a gas grill or BBQ. You can also make these in the shape of a rissole and pan fry. Serve this recipe with one or two of the dips from the 'Dips and spreads' section and with any of the green salads from the 'Fresh salads' section. Serves 6-8 people.

Char grilled corn and potato

Ingredients

4 large washed and peeled potatoes (800 g)

3-4 corn cobs, cut into sections or whole

Salt to taste

This is so simple and a great way to cook these two everyday vegetables and turn them into something exciting and tasty.

Slice the washed and peeled potatoes long-wise into 5-6 mm thick flat discs and salt if desired. Cook on an open grill over a wood fire or gass grill or BBQ. The surface of the potatoes should go a golden brown and blister when cooked. At the same time you are cooking the potatoes throw a few fresh juicy cobs of corn on the side. Be careful that the fire is not too hot, as it might burn the surface of the vegetables before cooking them through. You will need to monitor them with care and attention and turn them regularly. Once cooked, serve the potatoes with the 'Chilli dipping sauce' (see page 33) and the corn with butter.

You can also cook sliced eggplant alongside the potato. Peel a large eggplant and slice into rounds 5-6 mm thick. This time, salt the eggplant and let it sit for 15-20 minutes so that the salt draws out the moisture. Then pat dry and rub off the salt before cooking alongside the potatoes. Serves 6-8 people.

Healthy vegetarian

Oven omelette, *Ijjie*

Ingredients

6 large eggs (65-70 g each)

2 cups onion (260 g chopped)

2 cups chopped Italian parsley (60 g)

3 cups grated marrow or zucchini (300 g)

1 level teaspoon white pepper (3 g)

1 level teaspoon allspice (3 g)

1 level teaspoon crushed rock salt (3 g)

½ cup plain flour (80 g)

Olive oil for frying

Using a whisk in a large bowl beat the six eggs and white flour and combine with the other ingredients and mix well. Pour the mixture into a greased oven pan or baking dish so that it is 2-2.5 cm thick (if your mixture is too high use a larger pan). Bake in a preheated oven at 180 degrees Celsius. Cut into slices as you would cut a pizza and serve with a salad. It also can be used for wraps with salad and cheese. Serves 4-6 people.

Lentil and rice pilaf

Ingredients

2 cups long grain rice (400 g)

2 cups brown lentils (400 g)

2 cups sliced onions (260 g chopped)

1 teaspoon rock salt (3 g)

1 teaspoon white pepper (3 g)

The appeal of this dish is in the combination of flavours using caramelised onion and lentils with the body of rice to bring it all together. It is a great summer dish served with a chilled fresh salad.

Cut the onions in halves and slice into thin semicircles. In a frying pan caramelise the onions using olive oil. Leave the onions aside in a bowl. In a deep pot add 4 cups of water, salt and pepper and bring to a simmer. Then add the lentils and rice, stir well and slow cook until the water is almost absorbed. Switch off the heat and place the lid on the pot and leave to sit for another 10 minutes while it finishes cooking. When the rice and lentils are fluffy, add the onions and mix well. Can be served hot or cold with a fresh side salad. Serves 4-6 people.

Silverbeet and chickpeas

Ingredients

5 cups chopped silverbeet (250 g leaf only)

2 cups cooked chickpeas

(may use tinned chickpeas)

2 large onions (300 g)

2-3 chopped chillies (optional)

1 clove garlic (5 g)

1/2 a lemon

1 teaspoon salt (3 g)

1 teaspoon white pepper (3 g)

Olive oil for frying

Steam the silverbeet until wilted and let it cool. With your hands squeeze the water from the silverbeet and lay it aside. Thinly slice the onions and caramelise in a large frying pan using olive oil. Thinly slice the garlic and add to the onions. Loosen the silverbeet and add to the pan and further fry for 2 minutes.

Drain the chickpeas and add to the pan and fry for another minute. Add extra olive oil if needed. To serve, garnish with sea salt, cracked black pepper and squeeze half a lemon on top. Serves 3-4 people.

Mjudrah, *lentil porridge*

Ingredients

2 cups brown lentils (400 g)

2 large onions (300 g)

¼ cup white rice (50 g)

1 level teaspoon rock salt (3 g)

Wash and cook the lentils in plenty of water until the skin is falling off. While the lentils are cooking, peel and slice the onions and fry in a pan using olive oil until caramelised. Drain the water from the cooked lentils and put to the side. Blend the lentils into a smooth paste using a blender or food processor. Strain the mixture removing any skins and place into a deep pan. Depending on how thick the blend is, add 1-1½ cups of the saved water back to the pan. Add the salt and pepper and slowly bring to a simmer. Once simmering add the rice and cook for 5-6 minutes until the white rice is cooked. You can serve this in a big dish or several small dishes and top with the caramelised onion. The mixture will set once it has cooled and is traditionally served cold.

Mjudrah, lentil porridge is traditionally served alongside a garden-style salad with fresh picked herbs. Lebanese food is known for its variety and its extensive use and love of vegetables. Although most of the dishes include lamb, the meals are often offset by a variety of vegetarian salads and dips like the recipes provided in the earlier sections.
Serves 3-4 people.

Felafel

Ingredients

1.5 kg soaked chickpeas

725 g of soaked broad beans

2 onions (350 g)

50 g peeled garlic

150 g coriander leaf

150 g fresh mint

150 g fresh parsley

15 g white pepper

Cumin powder to taste

15 g rock salt

2 litres grape seed oil or olive oil

One of the most popular Lebanese dishes around, the humble felafel even inspired the name of a famous Australian novel which was later made into a movie. Once you have learned how to make these properly you will never eat another packet version or even buy one from a kebab shop.

Soak 1 kg of dried chickpeas and dried broad beans for up to 24 hours, and use only what is required. The rest can be frozen for later use. If using unpeeled dry broad beans you will need to peel the softened skins off the broad beans before you can mince them. You may be able to find peeled broad beans in some Lebanese delicatessens. The chickpeas and broad beans will increase in weight by absorbing water after being soaked. You will only need 1.5 kg of soaked chickpeas and 725 g of the soaked broad beans for the mix.

Start by chopping the onion into 8 sections and pass all the ingredients - except the spices - through an electric mincer or hand-cranked meat grinder. Do not use a bladed food processor as this will spoil the texture. Once the beans, chickpeas, onion and coriander have all been ground up, add all the spices, except for cumin, and mix well. The mixture should have a grainy texture with specks of green throughout and should feel clumpy and moist. The quantities used in this recipe will make a big batch, take out what you want to cook and freeze the rest by storing it in an air-tight container.

At this stage add the cumin (around 2 teaspoons to half a kilogram of the mixture) and if you like your falafel a little spicy you can add a little chilli powder. Using your hands mould the remaining mixture into small balls around 3-4 cm in diameter, ready to be deep fried. Deep fry the falafel balls in a the grape seed or olive oil until golden brown. The cooked ball should be crispy on the outside but still moist and a little green in the middle. The trick is not to cook too many at once and not to cook them too long.

Falafel can be served with other mezza style food or you can have it with lettuce, tomato, and hummus rolled up in Lebanese flat bread. It is best when it is hot and served with hummus.

Fried plantain

Ingredients

4-5 green plantains

Chilli sauce

1 litre grape seed oil

for deep frying (olive oil optional)

This Ghanaian version of hot chips is made from plantain which is from the same species as the commercial banana and will go yellow and sweet if left to ripen. The plantain is starchier like a potato when green and can be fried in oil as you would fry potato. You can purchase plantain from Indian food stores that stock Fijian or Pacific island groceries.

Peel away the green skin and slice into rounds or however you prefer. Heat the oil until almost smoking and fry a bunch at a time. When frying, always remember not to crowd the oil as it will drop the temperature too quickly and the food you are cooking will not crisp.

Another version is to let the plantain ripen and go sweet and cook on a grill over an open wood fire. When the plantain have ripened, peel and slice into long sections - cutting along the length of the fruit The savoury chip version is served with chilli sauce or can be served with a meat or fish sauce; The ripened sweet version is excellent as a dessert similar to regular bananas and can be served with crushed unsalted peanuts and ice cream. Serves 3-4 people.

Green beans and tomato

Ingredients

4 cups fresh green beans (400 g)

3 large tomatoes (360 g)

2 large onions (300 g)

2 cloves garlic chopped (10 g)

1 tablespoon tomato paste (30 g)

1 teaspoon salt (3 g)

1 teaspoon white pepper (3 g)

Black olives for garnishing

This is a favourite vegetarian meal, similar to the 'Green beans with lamb recipe' (see page 49), but with no meat. My mother preferred the beans to be well cooked until they are a dark olive green colour. I prefer the beans to still be a little crunchy and firm.

Finely chop the onions and fry in a deep saucepan with extra virgin olive oil. Cook the onions until soft and then add the chopped garlic and stir. Cut the tomatoes into small chunks and cook in with the onions until the tomatoes are starting to break down. Add the salt and pepper to the mix. Give the mixture another stir and toss in the green beans. Add ½ a cup of water and a spoonful of good quality tomato paste. Cook until done, depending on how you like the beans. I normally cook for another 3-4 minutes after I add my beans.

This recipe can be served hot or cold and garnished with some parsley and black olives. Serves 3-4 people.

Fried vegetables

Ingredients

1 whole fresh aubergine
(depending on size, around 500 g)
1 whole cauliflower (around 1 kg)
50 g salt
2 litres grape seed oil for deep frying cauliflower
Extra virgin olive oil for frying aubergine
Variety of dips and sauces from the
'Dips and spreads' section (see page 30)

This is a simple and tasty recipe that relies on the freshness of the raw vegetables and their preparation for their taste.

To prepare the aubergine you will need to firstly peel it and slice into thin sections along the length, around 6 to 8 mm in thickness. Place the sections in a large flat tray and salt with plenty of salt and let sit for 1½ hours. You will notice that the salt will drag away the moisture from the flesh of the aubergine. With a dry, clean tea towel, dust off all the salt and dry each section and place on a dry tray ready to fry. To prepare the cauliflower all you need to do is snap the trees off in a medium section, around 4-5 cm canopies. The very large pieces you can cut in half. Rinse the pieces and dry well so to avoid any water in the hot oil. When you have prepared all the vegetables, you are ready to start cooking.

To fry the slices of aubergine use a non-stick frying pan to avoid using to much oil. You will need a pan large enough to cook 2 to 3 slices at the same time. Heat the pan and add enough extra virgin olive oil to coat the surface of the pan. Fry one side then turn over and fry the other side. The slices should go golden brown and become soft and tender. You will notice that the aubergine soaks up the oil like a sponge, so avoid adding too much oil.

Deep fry the cauliflower in grape seed oil. The grape seed oil has a higher boiling temperature than most oils and browns quicker. You will need around 2 litres of grape seed oil in a deep pan. Heat the oil until it is almost smoking and start cooking. Do not add too many cauliflower pieces as this will drop the temperature of the oil too quickly. For the first batch you will need to back off the heat a little so that they do not brown too quickly. Once all the pieces are cooked you can serve both vegetables together with a selection of salads, sauces and dips.
Serves 4-6 people.

Fermented corn dumplings

Ingredients

500 g polenta (2 packets)

2 cobs fresh corn

3 cups water

Husks from 4-5 corn cobs

Food grade raffia or cotton twine

Corned beef chilli sauce (see page 62), or

Chilli fish sauce (see page 118)

This Ghanaian recipe is traditionally made with a coarser ground maize which is now available in African grocery stores around Australia. When my family arrived in Australia these stores had not opened, so my mother used the closest thing available which is polenta. These dumplings are made from a fermented corn dough and are served alongside several types of sauce. The Fermented corn dumplings are served with a spicy corned beef sauce and a similar sauce made with fish, which is my personal favourite.

Place the water and polenta in a large glass bowl and leave to sit uncovered on the kitchen bench in sunlight for a minimum of 2 days. This will start the fermenting process and the corn will go sour. On the third day add the fresh kernels from the two corn cobs and stir in. Place the contents of the bowl into a large pot and bring to a simmer; stirring constantly. Cook for 4-5 minutes and add water if the mixture is too dry. Be careful not to let the corn stick or burn by constantly stirring as you cook. Once you have cooked the corn for around 5 minutes put aside and allow to cool until the mixture can be handled.

The next part is the fun part like wrapping Christmas presents. You will need the inner leaves of the corn cob to wrap with and raffia or twine to tie the parcel. Select around 100 grams of the corn mix and squeeze any excess water out, forming a ball in your hand. Place the corn ball on a leaf as shown in the top inset photo. Roll the leaf around the ball of corn as shown on the second inset photo. Then place the packet on another leaf as shown in the third inset photo and wrap around the packet as before - enclosing the corn. Tie with raffia or cotton twine as if you were wrapping a present. Trim the excess raffia after the knot. Repeat for all of the corn mix.

Once this is done, they are ready to boil. Place enough water in a large pot to cover the parcels and bring to a simmer. Once the water is boiling, add the dumplings and cook for 45 minutes to 1 hour. If you do not want to cook it all, simply freeze the remaining corn mix for another time.

Seafood

Fried garfish

Ingredients

6-8 fresh garfish, (bream or red-fin bream optional)

flour to dust with (300 g)

1 litre grape seed oil (olive oil optional)

1 packet of Lebanese bread (6 - 7 pockets)

My parents were not great consumers of seafood but still indulged in a few favourite recipes. Seafood was kept very simple and in most cases baked or fried. The following recipes are the ones that my mother mostly made and these were cooked on the weekends when my father would go to the markets and buy fresh fish. The first recipe uses garfish, if you can't find garfish use bream which is another coastal fish of Lebanon. My father would also purchase fresh prawns to be cooked alongside the fish.

To cook the garfish deep fry them in grape seed oil. You can use a mix of half olive oil and half grape seed oil if you prefer a different taste. The grape seed oil is a hotter oil and will crisp the fish much better than olive oil. Make sure that the garfish are cleaned and gutted then dusted liberally with the flour and put aside.

In a large deep pan, big enough to fit 3 to 4 fish, pour in the litre of oil and heat until it is almost smoking (I use a wok on a gas burner and cook the fish outside). Fry 2 or 3 fish at a time so that you do not cool the oil too quickly. These fish will cook very quickly because they are not very big. It should take no more than 3-4 minutes for each fish to be golden brown. Cook all the fish in the same way.

Every time we cooked fish, it was a tradition to fry some bought flat Lebanese bread with the same oil before it went cold. To do this we separated the pocket into two halves and dipped each section flat into the oil. Your pan must be big enough to do this or the bread will fold over itself. This will brown very quickly so you must be quick to pull out the half section of bread and let the oil run off back into the pan. Once you have cooked three to four halves, place on a large platter and put the fish on top of the bread, garnish with some green and red salad vegetables and it is ready to serve.

The best sauce to serve with fried garfish is tahini sauce and my all time favourite chilli sauce. Recipes for both can be found in the 'Dips and spreads' section at the beginning of the book.

Serves 3-4 people.

Fried prawns

Ingredients

Quantity of prawns to suit the
number of people being served
1 litre grape seed oil (olive oil optional)

*This is as simple as it gets with seafood. Start by
purchasing the freshest green prawns you can find
from the fish markets or a good quality seafood outlet.
Make sure they are a good size, not too small or too
large. When you have purchased the prawns wash
well, drain and place aside. If you are fussy about the
shell you can peel it away but traditionally we do that
later after the prawns are cooked.*

If you have an outdoor cooker it is best to cook the
prawns outside avoiding oil splashes. I use a large
wok on a big gas burner outside. Depending how
large your pan is, put 4 to 6 prawns in the hot oil and
cook for around a minute or less. If they are a smaller
variety, you can add a few more. When removing
from the hot oil make sure you drain the prawns well.
Drain any remaining oil from the cooked prawns by
sitting them on paper towels before serving. Cook the
remaining prawns in the same way.

This prawn recipe would go well with the garfish as a
seafood combination. You can also fry some eggplant
and cauliflower in some fresh oil and serve as a side
dish. A good salad choice to serve with the prawns
is 'Fattoush' (see page 22). Fattoush has a complex
tangy fresh flavour from the sumac and lemon juice
which will work well with the seafood flavours.

A good combination of sauces to serve with seafood
is 'Tarator' sauce' and 'Chilli sauce' (see page 33).
To make 'Tarator', which is the Lebanese version of
tartare sauce, add 20 g finely chopped parsley to the
'Tahini dressing' (see page 18). Another suitable salad
to serve with fish is 'Cauliflower salad' (see page 28).

These recipes make a great seafood mezza cuisine
spread, served with chilled white wine and eaten
outdoors on a clear sunny day with friends. They are
easy to prepare and quick, simple but very delicious.

Baked fish with saffron rice

Ingredients

1 kg whole fish cleaned and scaled
(snapper is my personal choice)

1 cup tahini dressing (220 g) (see page 18)

1 large onion sliced into rings (160 g)

1 medium onion sliced into half moons (130 g)

1 medium to large lemon

for saffron rice

¼ cup pine nuts (30 g)

2 cups washed rice (400 g)

1 teaspoon salt (3 g)

¼ teaspoon powdered saffron

2 litres boiling water (8 cups)

Combined with fried vegetables, fresh salads and the saffron, this fish recipe rice makes a great centre piece for a special dinner party. You can be very creative in the way you prepare and present the fish by adding colour with basic ingredients such as parsley, tomato and capsicum.

Brush the fish with olive oil and salt: inside and out. Thinly slice round shaped lemon pieces and put the slices into the fish. Place the fish on a non-stick baking pan and cook until the flesh becomes opaque and flaky. A fish weighing around 1 kilogram should take no more than 20 minutes. Remember that the residual heat in the pan will keep cooking the fish for a few minutes more after you remove it from the oven. I constantly monitor my fish and always remove it just before it is done and let it sit for a few minutes.

While the fish is cooking, sauté the onion rings in a pan using olive oil until they are just starting to brown and put aside to cool. When these have cooled, mix them into the tahini sauce. Slice the rest of the lemon into wedges to garnish the fish.

Place the tahini sauce with the onion onto the platter you are using to present the fish as this will become the base. Once the fish is cooked, carefully remove from the baking pan and place on top of the sauce in the centre of the plater. Garnish around the fish with some sliced capsicum for colour and sprinkle parsley over the sauce. Place the lemon wedges on top of the fish. Voilà! There you have it.

To make the saffron rice begin by browning the pine nuts in a small pan and put these aside. In a saucepan sauté the onion sliced into half moons until they begin to brown and then add the washed rice and salt allowing these to cook for a couple of minutes whilst stirring. Pour in three and a half cups of boiling water and add the saffron. Stir and bring to a simmer, half covering the pot with the lid. Cook until all the water has evaporated and the rice is tender. Serve on a platter with the pine nuts sprinkled on top. Serves 3-4 people.

Chilli fish sauce

Ingredients

Cod fillet (500 g)

1 medium onion chopped (130 g)

4-5 red chillies chopped (20 g)

1 teaspoon fish sauce

1 teaspoon white pepper (3 g)

1 teaspoon salt (3 g)

2 tablespoons tomato paste (60 g)

1 cup water

Fermented corn dumplings (see page 107)

This is a Ghanaian spicy fish sauce which you can make as hot as you like by adjusting the amount or type of chillies used. I have used a variety that are not very hot but have a good flavour. This sauce is simple and quick to make. You can make it with most types of white, flaky fish fillets, but I prefer to use cod. It is best served with 'Fermented corn dumplings', or simply with boiled white rice, potato, taro or cassava. These types of root vegetables including cassava, taro, and yams can be purchased from Indian food stores that stock Fijian or Pacific island groceries

In a shallow pan fry the onions in olive oil. While the onion is cooking cut the fillet of cod into large chunks and set aside. Prepare the sauce by adding the tomato paste to 1 cup of water and dissolve into a wet sauce. When the onions start to brown, add the teaspoon of fish sauce, chillies, salt and pepper to the pan. Then add the pieces of fish and cook for 1 minute, turning over each piece as it cooks. Stir in the sauce and simmer for a further 4-5 minutes.

As careful as you might be, the pieces of cod will break apart as you cook and stir the sauce, so do not worry about it too much as it will still taste fantastic. The sauce is ready when it has reduced into a thick rich consistency. Serve alongside a few fermented corn dumplings and enjoy the simple flavours of traditional African food. The fermented corn dumpling recipe can be found in the vegetarian section of the book.

Another version of this recipe can be made with tinned fish such as herring or sardines. This is an option you can try if you are unable to find fresh fish. I have tried both and recommend that you stick with fresh fish. The essence of this sauce is to provide an accompaniment to the sour corn dumplings; this is a typical theme in African cooking. African food contains many root and starch vegetables as the basic staple. Depending upon which region, and the season these recipes will vary, but essentially the concept is the same. Serves 3-4 people.

Game meat

Dukkah duck

Ingredients

1 whole duck (2-2½ kg)

40 ml fresh lemon juice

40 ml virgin olive oil

2 cloves garlic (8 g)

Dukkah (80 g)

dukkah (makes enough for duck and stuffing)

¼ cup sesame seeds (40 g)

½ cup pine nuts (80 g)

2 tablespoons dry oregano leaf (8 g)

¼ cup coriander seeds (20 g)

4 teaspoons ground cumin (8 g)

½ teaspoon chilli powder

1 teaspoon white pepper (3 g)

2 teaspoons cinnamon (½ g)

2 teaspoons allspice (4 g)

stuffing

½ cup bread crumbs (50 g)

½ cup almond meal (50 g)

2 tablespoons dukkah (20 g)

½ chopped onion (80 g)

I still remember the first time my father took me hunting. He sat me on a log near a dam where two wild ducks were swimming, then instructed me on how to hold and aim the gun. He then said, 'slowly squeeze the front trigger', I did as he said and the recoil pushed my finger onto the next trigger and both barrels went off. I toppled backwards as my father burst out laughing but got the duck! You can use wild duck from a game meat supplier or the commercial variety found at butchers and supermarkets. I have used the commercial variety which takes around 45 minutes to cook per kilogram.

Using a blender, blend the dukkah ingredients into an even consistency. This will make enough for the marinade and the stuffing. Prepare a marinade for the duck by crushing the garlic cloves into a fine paste using a mortar and pestle, then add the lemon juice, olive oil and 80 grams of the dukkah and set aside. Mix all the stuffing ingredients together and add a little water or olive oil so that it combines and set aside.

Prepare the duck by removing any internal organs and trimming the excess fat and skin around the cavity then dry with a paper towel. Rub a handful of the stuffing inside the duck, patting down flat the remainder that falls of the walls, keeping the cavity open and clear, do not overfill or close the cavity.

Using a sharp knife score the body of the duck just cutting through the skin in a cross hatch pattern, this will allow the skin to crisp. Liberally rub the dukkah marinade all over the duck. Cross over the legs and tie together with twine. Fold the wing tips back under the upper wing, the duck is now ready to cook..

Put the duck on a wire drip tray inside an oven tray. Preheat the oven to 220 degrees Celsius and cook for 10 minutes, drop the heat back to 180 degrees Celsius, cook for another 40 minutes. Using the fat from the duck lightly brown your potatoes in a frying pan and then add them back to the oven tray. For the last 40 minutes drop the heat to 140-150 degrees Celsius, monitoring to make sure that the skin is crispy, the flesh moist and not overcooked. Serve with gravy or any of the salads from the 'Fresh salads' section of the book. Serves 3-4 people.

Spiced quail

Ingredients

4 medium quails (150 g each)

¼ teaspoon white pepper (1 g)

¼ teaspoon salt (1 g)

¼ teaspoon cumin (1 g)

¼ teaspoon allspice (½ g)

Pine nut sauce

¾ cup pine nuts, mashed into a fine paste (80 g)

Butter (30 g)

½ cup milk (100 ml)

1 tablespoon white flour

Mashed potato

4 medium potatoes (peeled and boiled)

3 hard boiled eggs

½ teaspoon salt

½ teaspoon pepper

¼ cup extra virgin olive oil

Silverbeet with chickpeas

5 cups chopped silverbeet (250 g leaf only)

100 g cooked chickpeas

2 large onions (300 g, chopped into semicircles)

1 clove garlic (5 g)

1 teaspoon salt (3 g)

1 teaspoon white pepper (3 g)

This recipe is based on the lunches we took when we went hunting. Combining the spiced quail with the mashed potatoes, silverbeet and exquisite pine nut sauce makes an elegant and exotic meal. These flavours for me are full of memories.

Steam the silverbeet until wilted and let it cool. With your hands squeeze the water from the silverbeet and set aside. Caramelise the chopped onion in a large frying pan using olive oil. Thinly slice the garlic and add to the onions. Loosen the silverbeet and add to the pan and further fry for 2 minutes. Then add the chickpeas, cook and stir for another minute, remove from the heat and set aside.

For the mashed potatoes, using a fork coarsely mash the potato and eggs, adding the olive oil salt, and pepper, mix well and set aside. To prepare the quails, mix the spices, salt, pepper, cumin and allspice together and rub liberally all over the quails. Preheat the oven to 160 degrees Celsius and cook the quail for 20 minutes in a pan with a little olive oil.

While the quail is cooking, prepare the pine nut sauce in a small pan by first melting 30 grams of butter on a medium heat. Reduce the heat and mix in one tablespoon of flour, in a similar way to making a rue. While constantly stirring, slowly add the half cup of milk, turning the mixture into a white sauce. Adjust the thickness by either adding more milk or flour. Still stirring the sauce, combine the pine nut paste and adjust the consistency, stir and cook for 30 seconds then remove from the heat.

When the quails are ready, divide each into two halves by cutting down the middle with kitchen scissors and assemble the dish as shown using a food stack or as you desire. Serve with the pine nut sauce and a good chilled white wine. Serves 3-4 people.

Rabbit in white wine

Ingredients

1 whole rabbit (1-1.5 kg sectioned)

Fresh rosemary (8 g)

Fresh thyme (6 g)

Fresh tarragon (8 g)

2 cloves chopped garlic (10 g)

1 teaspoon salt (3 g)

1 teaspoon pepper (3 g)

3 cups white wine

½ cup chicken stock (100 ml)

3 eshallots (120 g chopped)

Swiss brown or portabello mushrooms (300 g)

White flour to dust with

2 x 30 g pieces butter

40 ml olive oil

6 large chestnuts (130 g)

My mother would cook the rabbit brought back from the hunting trip the next day. Normally she would use common Lebanese spices, but sometimes she would do something different as with this recipe and use a French way of cooking the rabbit. This is a herbaceous, rich rustic dish with wine and mushrooms topped with roasted chestnuts, eaten with crusty bread.

Begin by sectioning the rabbit, removing the hind and fore legs and then cut the torso into even sections cutting perpendicular to the spine. Mix the 3 cups of wine, garlic and herbs to make a marinade, then add the rabbit pieces and refrigerate overnight.

When ready to cook, remove the rabbit pieces and clean away any herbs and garlic and pat dry with paper towels then dust with flour. Strain the 3 cups of wine removing the herbs and garlic, this will be added back to the rabbit at a later stage. Slice the mushrooms and have them ready. In a large frying pan using 30 grams of butter and 40 ml of olive oil, seal the rabbit pieces on high heat, turning them over a few times, remove and set aside. In the same pan reduce the heat and add the chopped eshallots and 200 grams of the mushrooms, saute for a minute and then add ½ a cup of chicken stock and ½ a cup of the strained white wine. Reduce for 5 minutes and then add the salt and pepper, stir and remove from the heat and set aside.

Put the sealed rabbit pieces in a large shallow dutch oven and cover with the mushrooms and eshallots. If you like, you can add extra fresh sprigs of herbs. Preheat the oven to 150 degrees Celsius, place the lid on the dutch oven and cook for 40 minutes. At the same time, pierce or slice the skin of the chestnuts and roast in a separate pan for 10 minutes alongside the dutch oven. Remove when cooked and let cool, then peel and slice.

After 40 minutes remove the dutch oven lid and let it cook for another 10 minutes. While the rabbit is cooking saute the remaining mushrooms, using the remaining 30 grams of butter. When ready to serve scatter the freshly cooked mushrooms and sliced chestnuts over the rabbit and plate up garnishing with some fresh herbs. Serves 3-4 people.

Venison kebabs

Ingredients

600 g venison fillet

3 cloves garlic chopped (15 g)

½ teaspoon salt (1.5 g)

½ teaspoon white pepper (1.5 g)

½ teaspoon allspice (1.5 g)

2 cups red wine (400 ml)

2 large onions (150 g)

2-4 large portabello mushrooms

6 x 30 cm long metal skewers

For this recipe you will need to find a good supplier of venison, someone who can supply top quality fillets and steak. Venison is a lean meat, and I have found, as my parents did, it is best to keep it simple. Being so lean, venison can handle a good marinade though; delicious served up as a main, char grilled marinated venison steak alongside tabouleh.

Begin by dicing your fillet, this amount should make six skewers. In a glass bowl, spice the meat and marinate in the red wine and garlic, cover with cling wrap and refrigerate overnight. When ready to cook remove from the refrigerator and let sit until the meat is at room temperature.

Cut the onions and portabello mushrooms into quarters and start assembling the skewers. Do this by placing a quarter of each mushroom and onion on each skewer evenly spaced between the meat. If you want to add some colour you can also use cherry tomatoes and capsicum. Once all the skewers have been assembled they are ready to cook.

As recommended with other kebab recipes in this book, cook the venison skewers on an open grill over a wood fire or on a gas grill or BBQ. The secret is to get the wood fire temperature right so that it char grills without burning the meat. Venison is lean and does not have a lot of fat and can be easily overcooked and dry if left too long. Cook the skewers for no more than 3-4 minutes, constantly turning them. With a basting brush using the leftover marinade, baste the meat skewers as you cook them. Serve with tabouleh or a garden salad. Simply delicious. Serves 3-4 people.

Desserts and sweets

Crème caramel

Ingredients

6 large eggs (65 g each)

½ cup sugar (150 g)

1½ cups milk (300 ml)

1½ cups cream (300 ml)

2 teaspoons natural vanilla essence

4 ramekins

caramel

¾ cup sugar (120 g)

½ cup water (125 ml)

In the 1920s, the French people played a major role in Lebanon by setting up the Constitution and establishing the government. During that period the French introduced many aspects of their culture to the Lebanese community. This is now evident through some of the food and even the Lebanese language. Beirut in its glory days was referred to as the 'Paris of the East', with its many French fashion stores, cafés and restaurants and other influences. Crème caramel is one of the those influences that has been adopted by the Lebanese as a favourite dessert.

Start by preparing the caramel to coat the ramekins. Mix ¾ of a cup of sugar with ½ cup of water in a medium saucepan, over a low heat and slowly bring to the boil by gently increasing the heat. Allow to boil and turn into a golden colour, being careful not to burn or dry the caramel out as it needs to be runny. Coat each ramekin, leaving around 3-4 mm of caramel at the base and set aside.

In a bowl, mix the six eggs with ½ cup of sugar and let sit for 5 minutes. Pour the milk and cream into a deep saucepan and heat until it is steaming - do not let the mixture boil. When it is starting to form a skin it should be hot enough. Let the milk and cream cool a little and then slowly add ¾ cup of the hot cream and milk into the eggs while whisking constantly. To this mixture add the vanilla essence and whisk. Then add the mixture back to the remaining hot cream and milk, whisking as you pour. Carefully fill each ramekin with the cream mixture, try not to disturb the caramel at the base of the ramekin.

Place the ramekins in a deep baking tray with water almost up to their lips. Preheat an oven to 165 degrees Celsius and bake for 30-35 minutes. Let the ramekins cool in the tray of water to room temperature. Run a thin knife inside the face of the ramekins and invert onto a dessert plate. The custard should slide out with the caramel pouring over the top. Serve as it is or with half a strawberry on top or even with a dollop of double cream. Serves 4 people.

Shortbread biscuits

Ingredients

500 g white flour

250 g ghee

150 g white sugar

2 teaspoons natural vanilla essence

12 peeled almonds

Baking can be so much fun and shortbread biscuits are popular biscuits crossing several cultures. These simple biscuits are traditionally cooked at Easter and Christmas but my family would occasionally make them throughout the year. Traditionally served as treats, these biscuits can be served after dinner or with morning or afternoon coffee and tea. As with traditional shortbread biscuits, the recipe is very simple, consisting mainly of flour and fat - the difference being that instead of using butter, the Lebanese use ghee.

In a mixing bowl mix the sugar and ghee, then and add the vanilla essence. Mix well and slowly add the flour - around ½ a cup - each time mixing and kneading as you add. When you have added all the flour, knead until the dough is silky and smooth.

Divide the mix into approximately 70 gram balls and pat into a disc shape using both hands. You should be able to make around a dozen biscuits. Place the biscuits onto a baking pan and push an almond in the centre on the top of each biscuit. If you do not have peeled almonds, take a handful of good quality raw almonds and soak in hot water for 1 to 2 hours prior to making the biscuit dough. Soaking the almonds will soften the skin on the kernel allowing you to peel it away easily.

When you have prepared the biscuits, place in a preheated oven and bake at 160 degrees Celsius until golden brown. Take out and allow to cool to room temperature. When the biscuits are cool, store in an air-tight plastic container and serve with tea or coffee or when guests and friends come to visit.

This basic recipe allows you to be adventurous and create your own interpretations; like adding dried raisins to the dough, or drizzling melted chocolate on top. You can put jam in the centre instead of the almond. This is the fun and creative part of cooking so experiment and have fun. Makes 12 biscuits.

Walnut pancakes

Ingredients

2 teaspoons dry yeast (16 g)

1 teaspoon sugar (4 g)

1¼ cups warm water (250 ml)

1½ cups plain flour (200 g)

2 cups finely chopped walnuts (240 g)

3 tablespoons sugar (45 g)

2 teaspoons cinnamon (8 g)

Icing for dusting

1 litre grape seed or olive oil for deep frying

This is truly a luxurious dessert worth serving after a nice dinner. Served with ice-cream or double cream, it is spicy but not too sweet and a great way to end a meal with family or friends.

Begin by dissolving the yeast and sugar in a ½ a cup of warm water and let stand in a warm place for at least 10 minutes, until it is bubbling. In a mixing bowl sift the flour and make a well in the middle, pour in the yeast mixture and gently mix into the flour. Pour in the remaining warm water and mix into a batter, the same consistency as pancake batter. Allow to sit for an hour.

While the batter is resting, prepare the filling by mixing the crushed walnuts, sugar and cinnamon in a bowl. This will be used as the filling for the pancakes.

Grease a flat non-stick pan (use a pancake pan if you have one) with a little oil and put on a moderate heat. Pour some of the batter into the pan so that you have a pancake of around 14-15 cm in diameter. Lightly brown one side leaving the top slightly wet and sticky. Do not cook the pancake all the way through, remove onto a flat surface remembering not to stack them on top of each other. Place 2 or 3 tablespoons of the walnut mixture on the wet side of a pancake and fold over to make a half moon. Seal the parcel by pressing the sticky outer edge together. Do the same to the remaining pancakes.

Once all the pancakes have been filled and sealed you can crisp them by deep frying each in a pan of hot oil - one at a time - until golden brown. Using a high temperature oil, such as grape seed oil, will make sure that the pancakes crisp quickly. Each pancake should take under one minute to crisp. Remove and drain well on a paper towel. Dust the tops liberally with icing sugar.

You can serve the crispy walnut filled pancakes hot or cold with ice cream or double cream. Leftover pancakes make a deliciously special morning or afternoon treat with coffee or tea. Serves 3-4 people.

Syrup
dough balls

Ingredients

2 tablespoons dry yeast (16 g)

3½ cups plain flour (400 g)

2½ cups warm water (500 ml)

1 teaspoon sugar (4 g)

for the syrup

2-3 cups white sugar (540 g)

½ a lemon

2 tablespoons rose water

2 tablespoons orange blossom water

2 litres of grape seed oil or olive oil for deep frying

This is the Lebanese version of doughnuts which are cooked on special occasions, such as parties, feasts, and holidays. As with the shortbread biscuits recipe (see page 132), you can create your own interpretation, by using different glazes and toppings. The floral waters used in this recipe can be purchased from a Greek or Lebanese delicatessen.

Prepare the yeast by dissolving it into ¼ cup of warm water, adding the teaspoon of sugar and allow it to rise and bubble for around 10 minutes. In a large mixing bowl sift the flour and make a well in the centre. Add the remaining warm water to the yeast and gradually add to the flour as you constantly mix into a batter. Cover the batter with a damp clean tea towel and let it rise in a warm place for 1½ hours. In the first hour, mix the batter at intervals of 15 minutes and let it rest for the last half hour. The batter will be smooth and elastic.

In a deep saucepan prepare the hot oil. To test for the correct temperature add a tablespoon of the batter into the hot oil. It should expand and rise to the top if the temperature is right.

I have found the best way to cook these balls is to use a piping bag with a large plain nozzle. Fill the piping bag up with the batter and cork the end. You will need kitchen scissors to cut the batter as it extrudes from the bag. Carefully hold the bag over the hot oil, but not too high or it will splash. Gently squeeze the batter out and cut the batter into around 4-6 cm lengths. Depending on the size of your pot of oil, cut enough sections to float separately and not stick together. Cook until golden brown, then remove and drain on paper towels.

To make the syrup, dissolve 2-3 cups of sugar in a saucepan and bring to the boil, squeeze in the juice of half a lemon and add the rose and orange blossom water to the mixture. Reduce until it is a syrup, remembering that when it cools it will thicken. Coat the golden dough balls with the syrup. For a twist you can dip the balls half way into molten dark chocolate. Serve with a sprinkle of cinnamon. Serves 6-8 people.

Walnut and minced date cakes

Ingredients

1 kg of coarse semolina

300 g unsalted butter

2 teaspoons yeast (8 g)

¼ cup sugar (45 g)

1 teaspoon mahlab (4 g)

2 tablespoons rose water

1 cup milk (200 ml)

for the walnut filling

250 g crushed walnuts

250 g crushed pistachio

½ cup sugar (90 g)

2-3 tablespoons rose water

for the date filling

500 g minced dried dates

These are popular Christmas and Easter holiday cakes which have two types of filling: walnut and minced date. The cakes are formed using special wooden moulds with a handle. You can purchase these from a Lebanese delicatessen. There are two shapes, a deep pyramid shape used for the walnut filling and a flatter, domed shape used for the date filling. If you do not have these moulds you can use your hands to make the shapes. The mahlab is a spice made from the seeds of a St Lucie Cherry and is also available from a good Lebanese delicatessen.

Melt the butter and mix in a large bowl, adding the semolina, yeast, sugar, rose water and mahleb. Rub the mixture together to form a short dough. Slowly add enough of the milk, a little at a time, until the dough becomes smooth and holds together. Leave to rest and rise for 1½ hours.

Prepare the walnut filling by mixing all the ingredients together in a separate bowl. Once the dough has rested take a small quantity - about the size of a golf ball - in one hand and shape into a ball. The size of the ball will depend on the size of the mould, adjust the amount of dough to the mould you have purchased. Punch a hole in the middle working in a hollow using your finger on your other hand. Once you have hollowed the ball, fill with the walnut filling and close the opening. Push the ball into the cavity of the pyramid mould flattening the base. To remove from the mould tap the edge of the mould on a table, holding your hand underneath the mould and the cake should pop out into your hand.

To make the date version, follow the same process. Make another batch of dough and fill with dates using the domed shaped wooden mould. Make sure the dates are minced well into a smooth, sticky, thick and dry jam. Once all the cakes have been prepared, bake in a preheated oven at 160 degrees Celsius until golden brown. Dust the walnut pyramids with icing and both cakes are ready to serve. This recipe will make more than enough for 6 people with plenty of leftovers which you can store in an air tight container to eat later.

After dinner treats

My family did not formally have dessert after dinner as such, but instead enjoyed sweets and savoury snacks on weekends, special events and when guests visited. If a guest was to arrive for a social visit we would offer them coffee or tea with a sweet or savoury snack that we had previously made, or on the rare occasion we did not have something home-made we would offer something of quality that we purchased and had on hand for such times. We were taught that it is always important to be hospitable and have something on hand to offer. My mother always had something in the kitchen or pantry, from a simple mix of home roasted nuts and pumpkin seeds to special sweets purchased from a Lebanese bakery.

The Lebanese people are world famous for their sweet filo pastries filled with nuts and cream. To make these sweets, like the ones shown in the photograph on the opposite page, you have to be a devoted and trained baker. I do not pretend to be able to make such delights and prefer to leave it to the masters. You can purchase a tray with an assortment of pastries and they will keep for a week as long as you have them sealed in an air-tight container. These can be an excellent after dinner dessert or a snack. Make sure you source an authentic Lebanese bakery with a good reputation. You may even be able to find a bakery that delivers online.

Growing up, instead of sweet filo pastries, we would normally have a spread of olives, cheese and fruit after dinner. Whether the fruit was fresh or dried, we always had fruit and olives in the house. If you do not want to make a dessert, offer your guests a combination of dried fruits such as figs and dates, fresh grapes, dried almonds, olives and halloumi cheese with some flat bread. What could be more healthy and tasty? This is an excellent combination to end a good meal.

Coffee and mint tea

Ingredients

Lebanese style fine
ground coffee

Sprigs of fresh mint

Lebanese or Turkish coffee pot

Lebanese or Turkish coffee cups
and saucers

For coffee drinkers, there is nothing more uplifting than the smell of fresh coffee beans and the aroma of freshly brewed coffee. My parents are coffee drinkers and every morning my father would wake before my mother and prepare a pot of Lebanese coffee. He would then wake my mother up and they would sit outside under the car port drinking coffee and planning their day. The aroma would float down the corridor and into the rest of the house. It was a wonderful smell to wake up to. So it is not surprising that I am seasoned coffee drinker.

Brewed coffee is so different to espresso Italian style coffee, it has a smoother, less acidic softer flavour and even texture. To make Lebanese coffee you can either find a Lebanese grocer or delicatessen who grinds and packs the traditional style dark to almost black roasted Arabica bean, or you can find a good European style coffee roasting house who can grind to the finest commercial setting. For the European substitute I personally use a bean blend using the Robusta bean which gives an added punch. It is a dark roast suitable for short blacks, and makes a good cup of Lebanese coffee.

Lebanese coffee is drunk using small coffee cups similar to the Italian espresso short black cups. They can be plain white or hand crafted and highly decorated. If you do find a Lebanese delicatessen who sells coffee you may also find that they sell the coffee cups and saucers. I searched online and found a Turkish handicrafts importer and purchased an exquisite set of porcelain cups and saucers. You can also find matching sets that include a decorated porcelain coffee kettle to decanter your brewed coffee into the little cups. This make an impressive and elegant formal coffee experience.

The coffee pots I recommend are made from stainless steel being more durable and easy to clean. I have three pots: two small and one large pot. One of the small pots is made from stainless steel while the other is a Turkish-style copper-coated pot. The large pot is made from stainless steel and holds around 500 ml and serves up to 5 cups each at 100 ml per cup on average. The smallest holds around 200 ml and serves up to 3 cups. The biggest pot is the most frequently used in my home.

The amount of coffee to water ratio is about 10:1, for 500 ml of water you would add 50 grams of ground coffee. This will produce a good cup of coffee, if you prefer it stronger just add more coffee. To brew the coffee heat the water until it begins to boil and remove from the heat before you add the coffee. If you add the coffee to the boiling water it will immediately rise and overflow. Add the coffee a spoonful at a time and stir, reduce the heat and slowly bring to a simmer, constantly watching and stirring. If the coffee begins to rise, the heat is too high. Stir and simmer for a minute and remove from the heat and let the coffee settle for 2 minutes, allowing the grains to sink to the bottom. If you are going to use your decorative coffee kettle, after brewing pour the coffee into the coffee kettle and let it settle. Then it is ready to pour.

When pouring either from the coffee pot or kettle pour gently into the cup and try not to shake or disturb the sediment at the bottom. Sweeten with sugar if you prefer but it is best without. Enjoy.

Making mint tea is a much simpler process and can be made using a conventional tea kettle or the same Lebanese coffee pots used to make coffee. This is more a herbal infusion than a traditional tea and is both remedial and refreshing. Mint tea is a good digestive and calmative. Simply boil 500 ml of water and take off the heat, add two or three 10-12 cm leafy sprigs of mint into the hot water cover and allow to infuse for 3-4 minutes before serving.

You can sweeten the infusion with sugar or honey if you like but I personally prefer it without. To be a little exotic serve the tea in a Moroccan tea glass. These glasses are also available from importers of Eastern kitchen goods and hand crafted products.

Mezza cuisine menus

Summer meal

A Lebanese mezza spread of specially selected dishes to suit a summer's day.

Salads and dips
Fattoush,
Oregano salad and
Hummus served with a
bowl of green olives.

Pastries
Sambousek with Chilli dipping sauce.

Lamb and rice
Chicken rice, with almonds
and pine nuts served alongside
Kebbe balls with yoghurt.

Cheese and fruit platter
Halloumi cheese, dried figs, dates, apricots,
raw almonds, fresh green grapes,
Lebanese coffee.

Saveur du Liban

A Lebanese mezza spread of specially selected Lebanese favourites.

Salads and dips
Tabouleh,
Broad bean salad and
Babba ghannouj served
with a bowl of green olives.

Pastries
Fatayer and Lahem ahjeen.

Lamb and rice
Rolled grapevine leaves,
stuffed with lamb and rice.

Cheese and fruit platter
Halloumi cheese, dried figs, dates, apricots,
raw almonds, fresh green grapes,
followed with Lebanese coffee.

BBQ banquet

A great outdoor BBQ banquet, combining fresh salads with smoky char grilled lamb.

Salads and dips
Aubergine and capsicum salad,
Tabouleh, Babba ghannouj,
and Hummus.

Char grilled potato
Char grilled thin sliced potato circles,
served with Chilli dipping sauce.

Lamb
Char grilled lamb skewers and
char grilled Lamb and red wine sausages.

Cheese and fruit platter
Halloumi cheese, dried figs, dates, apricots,
raw almonds, fresh green grapes,
followed with Lebanese coffee.

Phoenicians' catch

A seafood mezza spread.

Salads and dips

Fattoush,

Tarator served with

deep fried Lebanese flat bread.

Fried fish and prawns

Fried garfish served with Fried prawns.

Fish and rice

Baked fish with Saffron rice.

Cheese and fruit platter

Halloumi cheese, dried figs, dates, apricots,

raw almonds, fresh green grapes,

followed with Lebanese coffee.

Hannibal's feast

A mezza feast fit for the great Hannibal,

an ancient Phoenician hero.

Salads and dips

Tabouleh, Babba ghannouj,

Hummus, and Broad bean salad.

Pastries

Sambousek served

with Chilli dipping sauce,

alongside Fatayer and Lahem ahjeen.

Lamb, fish and rice

Chicken rice, Kebbe balls served

alongside Fried garfish.

Dessert and sweets

Crème caramel,

Walnut and minced date cakes,

followed with Lebanese coffee.

Vegetarian banquet

A healthy and tasty selection of vegetarian mezza

dishes that would also please any meat eater.

Salads and dips

Herb salad,

Cauliflower salad,

Hummus and

Broad bean salad.

Pastries and patties

Fatayer and

Falafel.

Rice and chickpeas

Lentil and rice pilaf alongside

fried Silverbeet and chickpeas.

Cheese and fruit platter

Halloumi cheese, dried figs, dates, apricots,

raw almonds, fresh green grapes,

followed by mint tea.

Winter warmer

A dinner that would warm and put a smile
on your face on any cold winter's evening.

Entrée

Mjudrah lentil porridge.

Main

Okra and lamb served
with Lebanese rice,
Rolled grape vine leaves and
Stuffed marrow, Kousa.

Dessert and sweets

Crème caramel and
Walnut pancakes.

Sweet pastry platter

Selection of sweet nut filled
Lebanese pastries served with
Lebanese coffee.

Yoghurt delight

Yoghurt based dishes combining the flavours
of lamb, yoghurt and Lebanese spices.

Entrée

Dumplings in yoghurt, Shish barak.

Main

Cracked wheat with yoghurt served
along side Kebbe in yoghurt.

Dessert and sweets

Crème caramel and
Syrup dough balls.

Sweet pastry platter

Selection of sweet nut filled
Lebanese pastries served with
Lebanese coffee.

Ghanaian banquet

An exotic feast exploring
different flavours and ingredients.

Entrée

Fried plantain with
Chilli dipping sauce.

Soup and dumplings

Palm soup with Foo foo dumplings.

Sour corn dumplings

Sour corn dumplings served
with Corned beef chilli sauce.

Tropical fruit platter

Sliced mango, bananas,
pineapple, guava, oranges
and white grapes.